# COMMUNITY DEVELOPMENT AS MICROPOLITICS

## Comparing theories, policies and politics in America and Britain

Akwugo Emejulu

To my mother,
Duane M. Emejulu,
and my grandmother,
Ollie Lee Mason

First published in Great Britain in 2015 by

Policy Press
University of Bristol
1-9 Old Park Hill
Bristol
BS2 8BB
UK
t: +44 (0)117 954 5940
pp-info@bristol.ac.uk
www.policypress.co.uk

North America office:
Policy Press
c/o The University of Chicago Press
1427 East 60th Street
Chicago, IL 60637, USA
t: +1 773 702 7700
f: +1 773 702 9756
sales@press.uchicago.edu
www.press.uchicago.edu

British Library Cataloguing in Publication Data
A catalogue record for this book is available from the British Library

Library of Congress Cataloging-in-Publication Data
A catalog record for this book has been requested

ISBN 978 144731 317 5 hardcover

Cover design by Liam Roberts
Front cover image kindly supplied by Liam Roberts
Printed and bound in Great Britain by CPI Group (UK) Ltd, Croydon, CR0 4YY
Policy Press uses environmentally responsible print partners.

# Contents

# About the author

Akwugo Emejulu is lecturer at the Moray House School of Education, University of Edinburgh, and co-director of the Centre for Education for Racial Equality in Scotland. Prior to entering academia, she worked as a community organiser, a participatory action researcher and a trade union organiser. Her research interests include the political sociology of race, gender and grassroots activism.

# Acknowledgements

This book was made possible by the support and encouragement of several people.

I would like to thank my doctoral supervisors Catherine Eschle and Rowena Murray at the University of Strathclyde for their unwavering support, commitment and expertise.

At the University of Edinburgh, I would like to thank Mae Shaw, Lyn Tett, Jim Crowther, Ian Martin, Sian Bayne, Jen Ross, Hamish Macleod and Rowena Arshad for providing a challenging and intellectually stimulating environment for me to flourish.

I am grateful to my academic colleagues further afield with whom I have had inspiring discussions about the themes of this book: Leah Bassel, Stuart Connor, Marjorie Mayo, Audrey Bronstein, Richard Freeman, Barry Checkoway, Tracy Soska and Robert Fisher.

I would like to thank the team at Policy Press for making the publishing process a joy.

My friends and family provided much needed support and good humour during the writing of this book. Many thanks go to Nnaemeka Emejulu, Ngozi Emejulu, Chika Emejulu, Elon Emejulu, Anaya Emejulu, Laura Emejulu, Chloe Puett, Lorena and Erasmo Gonzales, Mercedes Garcia, Lucy McEachan, Poe and Scotty McHugh, Mick Peter, Andrea and Edward Chapa and Sonia Ahmed.

My thanks to the following publishers for permission to make use of their material:

Emejulu, A, 2011, 'Can "the People" be feminists? Analysing the fate of feminist justice claims in populist grassroots movements in the United States', *Interface*, 3, 2, 123-51.

Emejulu, A, 2011, 'Re-theorising feminist community development: towards a radical democratic citizenship,' *Community Development Journal*, 46, 3, 378-90.

Emejulu, A, 2010, 'We are the ones we've been waiting for: community development, collective identity and agency in the age of Obama', *Community Development Journal*, 46, 1, 117-31.

Emejulu, A, 2010, 'The silencing of radical democracy in American community development: the struggle of identities, discourses and practices', *Community Development Journal*, 46, 2, 229-44.

# CHAPTER ONE

# Introduction: what are the micropolitics of community development?

Why is community development regularly invoked as a way of tackling social problems? Why do politicians and policy makers routinely call on community development to rebuild bonds and trust between different groups of people? What is at stake philosophically, politically and in policy terms when community development is championed as a strategy for social renewal? Through a comparative analysis of American and British community development since 1968, this book aims to examine how key political and policy debates about social justice and social welfare have been inscribed onto and embodied within the theories and practices of community development in America and Britain. I call the processes by which contentious macro-level debates about the causes and solutions to social problems are embodied within the narrower spaces of community development 'micropolitics' in order to spotlight the complex nexus of politics, policy making, professional practices and grassroots activisms that are the bedrock of community development. Analysing the micropolitics of community development can, I argue, help to shed light on some of the underpinning contradictions and dilemmas of community development and support critical approaches to community development theory-building and grassroots practice.

In this book I seek to do two things. First, through a comparative historical analysis of community development discourses in America and Britain since 1968, I attempt to examine the changing nature of community development and map the competitions and contentions between different conceptions and practices of community development in each country. Putting community development in a transatlantic and historical comparative context is a powerful way of trying to understand the genealogy of particular ideas, political identities and social practices within this field. American and British community development have distinct but interrelated intellectual and practice traditions and have had sustained dialogues, disputes and transfers of knowledge since the early 20th century. Exploring the convergences and divergences in theories, politics and policies between these two countries is one important way of analysing and understanding the implications of the micropolitics of community development. Second, I attempt to analyse the changing identities of community, practitioner and policy actors over time and in each country. Mapping the ways in which different actors, in various community development processes, are ascribed particular values and meanings is crucial for understanding the competing and often unequal ways in which community development operationalises its key concepts such as equality, empowerment and social justice in relation to particular individuals and groups.

Before turning to explore the micropolitics of community development in further detail, I want to first define and discuss some of my key concepts and explain my framework for identifying and analysing community development discourses across time and national contexts.

## Community development

One of the biggest challenges of writing about community development theory, policy and politics is the lack of consensus among practitioners, activists, policy makers and academics about what community development might actually be. Community development can legitimately be defined in a number of different ways reflecting competing ideals about democracy, social justice and equality and divergent analyses about the role of the state, the market and civil society in promoting the common good (for example see: Alinsky 1971; Jones and Mayo 1974; Fisher 1994; Popple 1995; Stall and Stoecker 1997; Naples 1998; Stoecker 2001; Henderson and Thomas 2002; Gilchrist 2004; Dominelli 2006; Shaw 2008; DeFilippis, Fisher, and Shragge 2010; Ledwith 2011; Beck and Purcell 2013; Ife 2013). Due to its pliable form, it is often difficult to discern what is being invoked (or silenced) when community development is deployed in discussions about social problems and solutions. Trying to discuss community development in a coherent way becomes even more difficult when it is placed in a comparative context. Attempting to tease out the meanings and purposes of community development in America and Britain, with each country's differing welfare state formations, citizenship regimes, activist and practitioner traditions and approaches to policy making further complicates matters.

Notwithstanding these considerable definitional challenges, for the purposes of this book I define community development as a 'political and social process of education and action to achieve self-determination and social justice for marginalised groups' (Emejulu 2010, 234). For me, community development is primarily about the contentious struggles between marginalised groups (those groups who are structurally disadvantaged politically, socially and economically due to their locations at disparaged and disrespected intersections of race, class, gender, ethnicity, disability and/or sexuality) and social welfare policy makers. From my perspective, community development is essentially a reformist process by which marginalised groups demand concessions from the state (and increasingly the market) to defend and/or expand social citizenship rights. What is particularly interesting and important about community development are the differing configurations it can take depending on how groups frame their political claims and collective identities. That community development can conceivably range from neighbourhood-level work to transnational coalitions makes it an important site for study and debate.

Interlinked with my definition of community development is my view that community development's primary organising principles are those linked to *social justice* and *social welfare*. I will now turn to briefly discuss each of these concepts in turn.

## Social justice

In social and political theory, social justice is primarily concerned with how a given society's 'social arrangements [are organised] that permit all to participate as peers in social life' (Fraser 2005, 5). Thus, social justice is about examining the nature of citizens' material resources, the quality of citizens' social relations and considering how these resources and relations might facilitate and/or undermine the practice of democracy. If citizens' resources and relations are predicated on gross inequalities in income and wealth and the inability to be respected by others, theorists argue that this undermines social solidarity and the ability for different groups to come together to define, debate and take action on the 'common good' (Rawls 1971; Young 1990; Fraser 1997). Social justice is typically understood as a two-pronged concept relating to the *redistribution of income, wealth and resources* and the *recognition of difference*.

The starting point for thinking about justice as redistribution is egalitarianism and the goal of creating a 'community in which people stand in relations of equality to others' (Anderson 1999, 289). Redistributive justice asserts that all humans are of the same moral worth and that all humans are moral agents. In other words, regardless of background, all humans are equal. For equality to be meaningful, however, all humans have an obligation to secure the equality of others. Thus equality is not just a passive state of affairs; equality must be constantly and actively fought for and secured by all for the benefit of everyone. According to theorists from the redistributive justice school, the greatest threat to equality is the unequal distribution of goods, services, jobs, wealth and income across different social groups. This inequality in distribution is an injustice for two reasons. First, inequality in distribution is an injustice in itself because it is unfair (Rawls 1971). In capitalist economies, inequalities in income and wealth are typically the result of the random chance of good and bad luck among individuals due to the operation of capitalism that creates economic 'winners' and 'losers' that concentrates income and wealth in an economic, political and cultural elite. Inequality in distribution is also an injustice because this inequality in material resources attaches itself to particular social positions such as class, race, ethnicity, gender, disability, geography and creates and re-enforces artificial and arbitrary social hierarchies. As a consequence of the concentration of wealth and resources at the top, this makes it extremely difficult for particular social groups to break out of cycles of inequality and poverty not of their making.

Thus the practical goal of redistributive justice is fairness in the distribution of the burdens and the benefits in a given society (Young 1990). While there is not space in this text to discuss this point in detail, redistributive justice is primarily concerned with how the state can intervene in markets to ameliorate the effects of the uneven developments of capitalism. Theorists argue that this is best achieved through an active welfare state funded by a tax and benefit system that redistributes wealth from the top to the bottom of the income brackets and the creation and support for good quality social welfare services particularly in the areas of education, health and housing.

Redistributive justice, however, is not the only way of conceptualising social justice. This is because the concept of redistributive justice does not effectively capture what is at stake when we think of 'public goods' that cannot be redistributed such as involvement in decision-making, participation in public life or whether specific groups and individuals are respected or seen as 'respectable' by others (Young 1990). As Benjamin and Emejulu (2012, 5) argue, justice as recognition:

> can be understood as the space that is created and the positive value that is attributed to different ways of being and different interpretations of social life. Recognition is about supporting, respecting and defending 'difference': those identities, cultures and social practices that are not

represented by the majority of the public or by dominant social norms.

The focus for struggles against the inequalities of 'misrecognition' is about understanding the ways in which status and privilege are unequally available to different groups based on how they conform to hegemonic ideals of what is constructed as normative. For instance, thinking about poverty as an injustice is not just about deprivation and inadequate living conditions, it is also about misrepresentations of 'the poor' in public life. As the most recent British Social Attitudes Survey (National Centre for Social Research 2013) demonstrates, the British public's attitudes to some people in poverty are starting to harden. This change in attitude can be partly attributed to media portrayals of people in poverty as feckless, workshy and scroungers even though this representation does not accurately reflect the actual experiences of those at the margins. Thus living in poverty is a twin injustice related to a lack of material resources and the lack of control over how one's experiences are portrayed and understood in the popular imagination. Understanding the injustice of misrecognition is important because this has an impact on quality of our debates about social problems and solutions. If some groups, due to their popular representations in public life, are not seen as valuable and legitimate members of society then they are highly likely to be excluded from public debates, decision-making and actions about the common good (Young 1997). Justice as recognition focuses on creating and affirming spaces for the differing (and often competing) views, perspectives and experiences of marginalised groups thereby countering the tyranny of the majority in democratic public life.

Although theorists tend to disagree on emphasis, it should be noted that the ideas of redistribution and recognition do not form a binary opposition within the concept of social justice, but are two sides of the same coin that seek to understand and address differing manifestations of inequality. In theory and practice, community development seeks to defend and expand the social justice claims of marginalised groups through both redistribution and recognition struggles. Redistributive acts often take the form of community participation/advocacy in the planning and implementation of social welfare services while recognition struggles can focus on issues of problem definition in policy making and the meaningful representation of systemically excluded groups in decision-making processes.

## Social welfare

Social welfare can be defined as organised intervention to tackle social problems and promote social well-being. For advanced capitalist economies, the state, through a tax and benefit system, is the primary actor for the planning and delivery of social welfare but third and private sector organisations are increasingly important players, particularly in America and Britain. 'Social welfare' embodies a set of collective ideals about the nature of a given society and it is through the provision of social welfare that these ideals are put into practice. Thus, compulsory primary and secondary education, social housing, universal healthcare, unemployment insurance and pensions all express a notion of social solidarity that citizens make to each other. In order to have a stable and democratic society in which citizens have equal opportunities to participate in public life, there must be social protections – in the form of social welfare – from gross inequalities.

A critical aspect to understanding the dynamics at play within the micropolitics of community development is the steady dissolution of the postwar welfare settlements in both America and Britain. Since the mid-1970s, the political consensus for Keynesian policies of full employment and comprehensive welfare for all has fractured and a new consensus has formed around free market capitalism[1]. In particular, the ideals and practices of social democracy have ceded to neoliberalism – an ideology of individualism underpinned by a logic of free market relations which champions competition, commodification and privatisation in individual and public life (Harvey 2007; Hall, Massey and Rustin 2013). Given that a key pillar of community development is the defense and expansion of social welfare and social citizenship, trying to understand transformations in the theories and practices of community development in this context of neoliberal hegemony is a key concern of this book.

---

[1]    To be sure, in the United States social welfare and the welfare state have never enjoyed the levels of popular public support and political consensus as seen in Britain and European social democracies more generally. The US is exceptional in both its resistance to the idea of welfare and its limited enactments of welfare provision particularly with regards to universal healthcare and income support. American intransigence regarding welfare is directly related to its particular form of race relations. Institutional efforts to thwart and subvert the advancement of African Americans' citizenship and rights has played a central role in retarding social solidarity and the development of its welfare state. (For a comprehensive discussion of this see: O'Connor 2008 and Sharkey 2012).

I will now explain my analytical framework for identifying and analysing community development discourses.

## Understanding community development as discourse

In order to analyse 'community development as discourse', I draw on insights from post-structuralist discourse analysis (PDA) and Lene Hansen's (2006) 'comparative moments' framework in particular. Post-structuralism asserts that language's primary function is not to describe reality but to ascribe meanings and value-systems about our identities and relationships (Derrida 1974; Foucault 1980; Howarth 2000; Laclau and Mouffe 2001). Words are not simply instrumental ways in which to communicate; they insert themselves between us and reality so that they convey specific cultural knowledge and 'truths' which discipline us to think, feel and behave in specific ways. Post-structuralist discourse analysis is concerned with understanding the construction and reproduction of identities within the language and practices of particular discourses through the analysis of talk and texts.

By 'discourse' I mean a structured system of meanings that ascribe individual and group identities and rules of expected behaviour (Derrida 1974; Foucault 1980; Howarth 2000; Laclau and Mouffe 2001). I use the concept of 'community development as discourse' because I wish to position community development as a social and political construction bounded by power relations, identities and social practices and contested by subjects seeking to preserve, oppose or transform their identities or the rules of behaviour. Studying the tension between how individuals are both subjects within a community development discourse – possible creators of their own identities – but also subjected to a discourse – their identities and behaviours are structured and ordered by dominant ways of interpreting reality – is a key concern for this book.

Using Lene Hansen's (2006) method, I selected and analysed 121 American and British community development texts dating from 1968 to 2000. My selection of these texts constitutes the primary data for my study. For the purposes of this book, I have defined 'texts' as books, journal articles, policy documents, practitioner training manuals, newspaper and magazine articles and speeches that constitute the discourses of community development. These texts have been selected based on their clear articulations of discourse and identity (they represent various schools of thought with regard to community development), they are cited widely by other texts (they are linked to other texts through extensive citations and similarities in their

7

articulation of ideas, concepts and catchphrases) and they provide a mixture of 'official' discourses (government policy on community development) and oppositional discourses (dissenting groups seeking to reconceptualise dominant ideas and practices important to community development).

I undertook my discourse analysis of community development using Hansen's three-step research method of:

1. Placing the community development discourses in a historical context by analysing the politically salient moments in which they were formed and structured
2. Identifying and analysing the language and practices of the community development discourses
3. Analysing the discourses' identity constructions of key community development actors

In terms of textual analysis, first I placed the texts in the context of three politically salient historical moments[2] that have significance for left-wing[3] politics in both America and Britain:

- the fracturing of the New Left from 1968 to 1975
- the rise of the New Right from 1979 to 1985
- the convergence of left–right politics from 1992 to 1997.

---

[2]    I discuss the significance and politics of each of these moments in greater detail in the following chapters.

[3]    I use the terms 'left-wing' and 'right-wing' as broad political categories that encompass a range of ideas and social practices. I do not mean to imply that contemporary political thought reflects a simplistic one-dimensional spectrum of political ideas or that the boundaries between right and left are so easily identified. Nevertheless, in the community development tradition, these labels are infused with meaning and convey important ideas about authentic grassroots practice. By 'left-wing' I include those political ideologies and practices that seek social justice in the form of the redistribution of wealth from rich to poor and the recognition difference in terms of identities among various groups (Young 1990 and Fraser 1997). By 'right-wing' I include those political ideologies and practices that seek to preserve the status quo in terms of economic and social hierarchies, oppose state-based remedies for economic and social inequalities and seek to use the state to defend and expand traditional morality and values (Klatch 1988 and Diamond 1995).

My choice of these three moments is underpinned by Hansen's principle that comparative moments should have 'political saliency'. In general, my decision to choose these three moments is driven by key transformations in left-wing political thought that heavily influence the rise of community development as a legitimate form of practice in marginalised communities in both America and Britain.

For the 1968 moment, as poverty was 'rediscovered' in the context of relative wealth in the post-war period, as new social movements were advocating for different kinds of social and political rights and as social science was being used as a tool for the rational state planning of social welfare, all of these developments helped to promote community development as a way of deepening democracy on both sides of the Atlantic (Calouste Gulbenkian Foundation 1968, 1973; Marris and Rein 1972; Loney 1983; Lemann 1995). In addition, 1968 and its legacy is often constructed in America and Britain as a transformative historical moment whereby the ideas of democracy, power and justice were radically transformed by the Civil Rights Movement, the New Left and the nascent second-wave feminist movement (Fisher 1994; Popple 1995). Perhaps it is easy to understand why the 1960s and early 1970s were seen as a 'Golden Age' of community development. In the US, the talk and action of both official state actors and grassroots activists was of participatory democracy, equality and a new type of freedom for various marginalised groups (Hayden 1961; Baker 1972; Piven and Cloward 1979; Gitlin 1995; Lemann 1995; Polleta 2005). In the UK, official state actors and socialist practitioners also had a high level of consensus about the role of the state to tackle various social problems (Calouste Gulbenkian Foundation 1968, 1973; CDP 1977, 1978; Loney 1983).

I selected the rise of the New Right from 1979 to 1985 because this moment also has important implications for community development. From about 1945 to 1975 a Keynesian consensus dominated the politics of America and Britain. There was a belief among state actors and the general public in the importance and utility of a programme of full employment and comprehensive welfare for all. (Fisher 1994; Lehmann 1995; Diamond 1995; Faulks 1998; Katz 2008). The double crisis of an oil-shortage fuelled recession, and the process of de-industrialisation, however, helped to spark a backlash against an activist and redistributionist state (Fisher 1994; Diamond 1995). This economic crisis also corresponded with a growing right-wing assault against the social democratic reforms of the previous decades (Fisher 1994; Diamond 1995; Katz 2008). Increasing unemployment, high tax burdens and what was perceived as a large and cumbersome state bureaucracy legitimised neoliberal tenets of a limited state, hyperindividualism and free enterprise (Piven and Cloward 1979; Golding 1983; Fisher 1994; Diamond 1995; Faulks 1998; Harvey 2007; Katz 2008). The mere existence of an organised and powerful opposition to left-wing politics is not what I think is most important about including this historical moment. It seems that this moment constitutes not simply a time of backlash and retrenchment. With the elections of Margaret Thatcher in 1979 in Britain and Ronald Reagan in 1980 in America, the closure of the state to left-wing influence and the dismantling of social welfare provision constitute a transformative event in both countries. Understanding the ideological triumph of the New Right in relation to community development is crucial and is connected to the final historical moment under scrutiny.

My selection of the convergence of left–right politics from 1992 to 1997 is also important for community development. The dominance of the New Right has meant that right-wing politics are often perceived as the 'common sense' approach, the standard by which other views and opinions are judged (for example of this see: Fukuyama 1990; Etzioni 1993; Giddens 1994). Community development, as I have defined it, is primarily a left-wing theory and social practice. Thus trying to understand how a left-wing theory and practice has fared during an extended time of right-wing political hegemony is essential. Furthermore, with the on-going crisis in socialist politics due to the collapse of the Soviet bloc and the breakdown of the New Left coalition due to 'identity politics', there was no effective opposition to the hegemony of the right during this moment in time (Faulks 1998; Katz 2008). For example, after being in opposition for more than a decade neither the Democrats in America nor Labour in Britain sought to reassert the spirit and legacy of social democracy but instead sought accommodation within the prevailing neoliberal consensus in order to make themselves more politically appealing to voters (for a detailed discussion of this see Faulks 1998 and Katz 2008). All of these developments need to be understood in relation to community development.

By spotlighting the philosophical, political and policy disputes at play in each of these moments, it is possible to better understand and contextualise the contentious micropolitics at work in community development over a forty-year period in each country.

I then analysed a range of community development texts to explore the various constitutive building blocks of competing community development discourses. I examined how the various discourses define and deploy a number of core concepts such as 'social justice', 'empowerment' and 'equality'. Understanding how particular definitions of key concepts become dominant or marginalised helps to explain how some meanings and definitions become taken for granted, uncontestable and are reproduced over time within the field of community development.

Finally, I analysed how the discourses construct particular identities by exploring how community development professionals, policy makers and community activists are ascribed particular values at different political moments in each country. Exploring how particular meanings and beliefs metastasise on particular identity constructions is an important way of evaluating the claims various traditions of community development make in relation to its key concepts such as democracy, justice, empowerment and equality.

With my key concepts defined and my research methods explained, I will now turn to discuss the organisation of this book.

## Organisation of the book

Chapter Two begins with a short overview of the post-civil rights landscape in America in 1968 in which civil rights activists were seeking to reframe the movement from civil to economic rights for African Americans. I then move to analyse three competing community development discourses linked to: the declining Civil Rights Movement; a resurgent populist movement inspired by Saul Alinsky; and the new technocracy administering President Lyndon Johnson's Great Society social welfare programmes. I argue that due to important changes in the nature of African American resistance, the competing Alinskyist and technocratic discourses come to dominate the theory and practice of American community development at this time. Consequently, the Civil Rights Movement's discourse and its attendant identities focusing on participatory democracy are silenced from the community development repertoire. This silencing of alternative conceptions of community development in the United States has, I argue, important implications for American theory and practice over the next forty years.

In Chapter Three I provide an overview of the debates regarding 'rapid social change' and the commitment of state action and resources to tackle key social problems in Britain in 1968. I identify two discourses for analysis: one linked, like in the American context, to the technocratic administration of the Home Office's Community Development Projects (CDPs) and the other constituted by those CDP practitioners in the field who developed a radical analysis of social problems and solutions. Departing from the usual narrative that is told about the CDPs, I argue that there are actually few significant differences between these two competing discourses because they share similar identity constructions in which the state is invested with agency while local people are constructed as passive objects to be acted on by the state and community development practitioners.

For Chapter Four, I return to the US in 1979. In the context of the growing influence of the New Right – a powerful coalition of social and fiscal conservatives – I argue that the remnants of the civil rights discourse, as represented in the anti-racist feminist discourse of this moment, are constructed as unfeasible and unfashionable by two dominant and competing community development discourses. These two discourses, constituted by 'non-ideological' populist community organisers and technocratic neoliberal professionals respectively, continue the pattern of constructing the community development professional with agency and local people as passive objects. Crucially, I also argue that it is at this time that community development begins to be used as tool for welfare state retrenchment by politicians and policy makers.

Shifting back to Britain during 1979 for Chapter Five, I begin with a short overview of the decline of traditional socialist politics and the twin rise of the New Right as embodied by the Thatcher government and post-Marxist politics as seen in feminist and anti-racist activism. In this complex space, community development practitioners compete to define the meaning of their field. One discourse is constituted by socialist professionals seeking to respond to a 'crisis' in left-wing politics due to declines in popular support for socialism and the subsequent rise and electoral success of the Right. In contrast, its competing discourse is constituted by 'non-ideological' professionals seeking to shift community development theory and practice away from radical utopian politics in order to make it more relevant to the politics of everyday life of working-class people. I demonstrate that both discourses adhere to and reproduce the familiar pattern in which the community development professional is the active agent while local people continue to be constituted as a passive object.

In my final chapter for the US, in Chapter Six I open with a short discussion of two important events taking place in 1997: the hegemony of the New Right coalition which forced the Democratic Party to shift to the right in order to become more politically appealing to voters and the divisiveness of so-called 'identity politics' which fractured left-wing politics throughout the 1990s. I argue that it is in this historical moment that we begin to see a new pattern emerging in opposition to the dominant identity constructions previously documented. In the discourse constituted by official state actors seeking to bring free-market principles to urban regeneration projects in poor neighbourhoods, I demonstrate how this discourse adheres to the established pattern of the professional invested with agency and local people constructed as passive. I argue, however, that in the competing discourse connected to coalition-building across different community groups, this discourse seeks to reclaim the previously marginalised civil rights discourse particularly in relation to participatory democratic ideals. This attempt to overhaul the dominant practices in community development since 1968 and create new democratic identities and spaces appears to be strongly associated with anti-racist feminism.

In Chapter Seven, my final chapter on Britain, I briefly discuss the legacy of the neoliberal project under the Thatcher and Major governments and examine its impact on the new Labour government in 1997. Similar to the US during this moment, we are starting to see fractures between the discourses in terms of identity constructions. In the discourse constituted by politicians and policy makers, it is seeking to transform the community development process into a neoliberal project promoting entrepreneurship for people living in poverty. This discourse follows the dominant pattern of identity construction in which the professional is invested with agency while local people are passive. Socialist, feminist and anti-racist practitioners seeking to construct community development as a process of developing critical consciousness constitute the competing discourse. Although this oppositional discourse partly follows the established pattern of constructing the professional as invested with agency, local people are now starting to be constructed as heterogeneous and with some ability to act.

In my concluding chapter, I discuss the meanings, purposes and practices of community development in the context of the on-going economic crisis and austerity measures in both countries. I argue that the crisis poses dilemmas for rethinking community development. In order to take democracy seriously, community development must help to drive a process of reclaiming the state as the key guarantor of individual and group equality, counter and subvert the neoliberal colonisation of community development civil society organisations and revive the tradition of community development as political education for social change. For community development to play an essential role in helping to undermine the privatisation of civic life, it must create spaces for collective deliberative dialogue and action.

CHAPTER TWO

# Community development in a post-civil rights America

## Introduction

This chapter focuses on the micropolitics of community development in the United States from 1968 to 1975; I have identified three discourses for analysis. The 'Democracy discourse' is constituted by the texts, language and practices of community organisers and activists of the Student Non-Violent Coordinating Committee (SNCC), an organisation which formed part of the militant wing of the Southern Civil Rights Movement. For the Democracy discourse, community development is constructed as a process by which to identify and support indigenous leaders to work towards progressive social change. In contrast to this, the 'Power discourse' is constituted by the texts, language and practices of Black Power and Alinskyist community organisers. For the Power discourse, community development is constructed as the way in which revolutionary vanguard activists inculcate an 'authentic' and essentialised sense of identity among 'the people'. Finally, in contrast to both the Democracy and Power discourses, the 'Poverty discourse' is constituted by the texts, language and practices of the bureaucrats administering the Johnson Administration's War on Poverty programmes. For the Poverty discourse, community development is constructed as a two-pronged process of reform in terms of democratising state-run social welfare programmes and reforming the culture of poverty among 'the poor'. I will begin this chapter with a short overview of the changing political and policy landscape that helped to form and structure the three discourses I have identified. I will then move on to discuss the structure and operation of each of the discourses and the contrasting identity constructions that each of the discourses constitute.

## 1968: the problematic transition from civil rights to economic rights

In order to understand the formation, structure and operationalisation of the community development discourses during this moment, I will discuss the growing uncertainty that was altering the politics of the

Civil Rights Movement during the mid to late 1960s. It is important to trace how the deterioration of the Movement helped create spaces for different ways of understanding poverty and inequality and new opportunities for the practice of politics. From the mid-19th century to the mid-20th century, the dominant form of African American resistance to social, political and economic inequality had been focused on attaining the formal political rights of citizenship: the right to vote, the right to protest, equal protection under law, the right to due process in the justice system, and so on (Hamilton 1974; Carson 1995: 9–19). This 'civil rights approach' was focused on achieving the goal of equal political participation in American society. The logic of civil rights leaders – from Frederick Douglass to Booker T. Washington to W.E.B. Dubois to A. Philip Randolph to Martin Luther King Jr. – was that enfranchising African Americans (particularly those living in the South) would make them a significant ethnic voting bloc, the patronage of which politicians of all stripes would have to win. Here is the historian Charles V. Hamilton (1974: 194) describing the political situation of African Americans after Emancipation:

> Blacks were not a political force to be reckoned with in the nineteenth and early twentieth centuries; therefore they could be ignored or their political progress delayed without discomfiture to the prevailing political order.

Thus the logic of civil rights was that by first building formal political power in terms of voting rights, this would help to secure *social citizenship* in terms of expanding African Americans' social and economic rights such as equal access to high quality education, employment and housing. This idea formed the basis of the modern Civil Rights Movement dating from the 1955 Montgomery Bus Boycott to the assassination of Martin Luther King Jr. in 1968. By the mid-1960s, the Civil Rights Movement had achieved a number of victories. The 1964 Civil Rights Act outlawed racial segregation in education, housing and public areas. This legislation mandated equal protection under the law for all citizens and was specifically designed to dismantle the Jim Crow apartheid system in the South. The 1965 Voting Rights Act[4] outlawed discriminatory voting practices by state officials – particularly those in the Southern states – that had prevented African Americans from exercising their right to vote. These twin legal victories, combined

---

[4]    Note that parts of the 1965 Voting Rights Act have been invalidated by the Supreme Court in *Shelby County v Holder* ruling in 2013.

with President Johnson's expansion of the welfare state in the form of his War on Poverty programme, were a landmark in American race relations. It is important not to underestimate the significance of the Civil Rights Movement's victories in these instances. These successes, however, highlighted problems in the logic of the Movement.

By 1965, the transition from 'civil rights to silver rights' (shifting protest from struggles over civil and political rights to social and economic rights) was proving problematic for the Movement (Raab 1966: 46). This is because when most successful social movements are institutionalised by the state, they find it difficult to maintain their momentum or to reorient themselves to new goals (Tarrow 1994: 142–6). By 1968, translating civil and political rights into social and economic rights for African Americans seemed all but impossible for the Movement. This problem was due to two inter-connected reasons: the 'leadership gap' in terms of effectively articulating demands for new rights, and a shift in the practice of black resistance in America. First, the leadership of the Civil Rights Movement was not designed to deal with the transition to demanding social and economic rights. Since the dominant politics of African American resistance had been focused on securing civil and political rights, the leadership was composed of two types of protest elites: lawyers and orators (Hamilton 1974: 192). Lawyers such as Thurgood Marshall (who, as part of the legal team of the National Association for the Advancement of Coloured People, helped to win the landmark 1954 *Brown v Board of Education* case and would eventually go on to become the first African American Supreme Court Justice) were geared towards elite battles with lawmakers and bureaucrats that focused on changes in the justice system and interpretations of Constitutional law. Orators such as Martin Luther King Jr. and John Lewis (who was chairman of the Student Non-Violent Co-ordinating Committee until his ousting in 1965) were designed for building a moral argument for the political equality of African Americans and disrupting the status quo through protest politics. Once political equality had been achieved in law, the leadership of the Movement did not have the capacity to transform into advocating for different kinds of rights. This leadership gap was recognised by Martin Luther King Jr. (1967, 158–9) in the year before his assassination:

> Many civil rights organisations were born as specialists in agitation and dramatic projects; they attracted massive sympathy and support; but they did not assemble and unify the support for new stages of struggle…We unconsciously

patterned a crisis policy and programme, and summoned support not for daily commitment but for explosive events alone.

By using the twin approach of legal arguments and non-violent direct action to push against a closed door to gain civil and political rights, the Movement finally broke down this door. The Movement leadership, however, was not well equipped to reorganise itself to start pushing against other closed doors related to social and economic rights. Here is John Lewis (1998, 364) reflecting on the problem of reorienting the Movement to these difficult new goals:

> We now had the right to vote. We now had the right to eat at lunch counters. We could order that hamburger now... *if* we had the dollar to pay for it... That was the challenge ahead of us now... We needed to deal with the subtler and much more complex issues of attaining economic and political power.

Thus, the crisis of leadership in the Movement helped to create a space for the transformation in the politics of black resistance.

As civil rights organisations struggled to reorient the Movement beyond formal political rights, the goals of African American popular protest were also shifting. Expectations of African Americans were raised with the passage of the Civil Rights and Voting Rights Acts, however, no substantive changes in the social, political and economic lives of African Americans were evident. Black people were still more likely to be living in poverty; unemployed or underemployed; living in substandard housing and subject to systematic police brutality in comparison to their white counterparts (Carmichael and Hamilton 1967, 33–39; Kerner Commission 1968, 7–20). The slow pace of change (and in many cases, the lack of any change at all) in terms of social and economic equality led to two interrelated problems: an increase in violent rebellion and an increased sense of futility in participating in formal politics. Thus at the very moment when Black people finally secured enfranchisement, there was a popular turning away from that type of political practice to other forms of protest. For example, in response to persistent economic inequality and police brutality, a string of urban riots broke out across America starting in 1964 (the same year the Civil Rights Act was passed by Congress), which then peaked in the wake of Martin Luther King Jr.'s assassination in 1968

(Carson 1995). Here is an interesting framing of the riots by a liberal social commentator during this time:

> A recipe for violence: Promise a lot; deliver a little. Lead people to believe they will be much better off, but let there be no dramatic improvement. Try a variety of small programs, each interesting but marginal in impact and severely underfinanced. Avoid any attempted solution remotely comparable in size to the dimensions of the problems you are trying to solve. (Wildavsky 1968, 8)

This rejection of the non-violent strategy of the Civil Rights Movement through mass rioting was linked to the growing perception of the illegitimacy of the existing political institutions. Because there did not seem to be the same sense of urgency on the part of the federal government and white America to tackle African American economic inequality as there was in securing basic political rights, many African Americans began defining the current political establishment as the main obstacle to revolutionary change in American society. For example, here is Lewis (1965 quoted in Lewis 1998, 363) articulating his frustration about the lack of change in the economic lives of Black people in days after the passage of the Voting Rights Act:

> The lack of concern on the part of the American public and the lack of concern and courage of the federal government breeds bitterness and frustration. Where lack of jobs, intolerable housing, police brutality, and other frustrating conditions exist, it is possible that violence and massive street demonstrations may develop.

Thus 1968 is a moment of transition when an influential form of politics – nonviolent direct action – was moving out of favour and being replaced with violent struggles and a growing sense of disillusionment with establishment politics[5]. In terms of community development, we can see these broad debates about social justice and social citizenship

---

[5]    Although this is not a focus of the book, it should be noted that the Federal Bureau of Investigation under the leadership of J. Edgar Hoover, systematically spied on and sought to subvert the Civil Rights, anti-war and student movements through the domestic espionage Counter Intelligence Program or COINTELPRO (for an excellent discussion of COINTELPRO see Weiner 2012).

playing themselves out in the formation of the three discourses I have identified for analysis. The militant wing of the Civil Rights Movement took a particular approach to community development through the process of identifying and supporting local leadership to organise non-violent protest activities and voter registration drives. As I shall demonstrate, the Democracy discourse is formed and structured by these practices and was moving out of favour during this moment in time (Baker 1960, 1972; Hayden 1961; SNCC 1963 ; Zinn 1964; Payne 1989, 2007; Mueller 1993; Carson 1995; Polletta 2003, 2004; Ransby 2003). The shift away from the strategy and tactics of the Civil Rights Movement and the reconceptualisation of community development as a populist process of building power for disenfranchised groups helps to form and structure the Power discourse (Alinsky 1971; Carmichael and Hamilton 1967; Carson 1995; Ransby 2003; Polletta 2003, 2004; SNCC 1968). Finally, the technocratic planners of the welfare state seeking to define community development as the process expanding federal social welfare programmes and the participation of poor people in service planning and delivery as set out in Johnson's War on Poverty programme, helps to form and structure Poverty discourse (Marris and Rein 1972; Brager and Specht 1973; Lemann 1995).

To fully appreciate the influence of these events on the discourses I have identified, however, I will now turn to analyse each of the discourses and their particular constructions of identity. I will begin first with the Democracy discourse and its constitution of a militant identity.

## The rise and fall of the Democracy discourse

> Black people who were living in the South were constantly living with violence. Part of the job [community organising] was to help them to understand what that violence was and how they in an organised fashion could help to stem it. The major job was getting people to understand that they had something within their power that they could use and it could only be used if they understood what was happening and how group action could counter violence even when it was perpetuated…by the state. (Baker 1972, 347)

The Democracy discourse is constituted by the ideas, language and practices most closely associated with the Student Non-Violent Coordinating Committee (SNCC) and its conception of participatory democracy. SNCC is a key subject and producer of the Democracy discourse because its identity and practices of community organising

20

for civil rights helped develop and sustain a successful social movement leading to key legislative and political reforms such as the 1964 Civil Rights Act, the 1965 Voting Rights Act and the expansion of the welfare state (for example see: Mueller 1993; Carson 1995; Ransby 2003; Polletta 2004; Payne 2007). For the purposes of this book, however, SNCC's role in legislative changes is perhaps less important than its influence on the thinking and practice of radical democracy and community development. SNCC was founded and sustained by Southern Black students and engaged in organising poor, working and middle class African American young people to demand civil rights by undertaking high profile non-violent direct actions to bring national and international attention to the American apartheid system (Carson 1995; Ransby 2003; Polletta 2004). Through its practices of working with marginalised and disenfranchised groups, SNCC sparked a new way of thinking about the construction of radical identity and the organisation of spaces to struggle for progressive social change.

Understanding the construction of participatory democracy in the Democracy discourse is important because this concept distinguishes the Democracy discourse from other competing civil rights discourses which focus on charismatic leadership or expert-driven development. Participatory democracy is defined as the belief that ordinary people have the knowledge, skills and capacity to deliberate, make decisions and take action on the issues that affect their lives (Baker 1960, 1–2; Hayden 1961, 3–4; Carson 1995, 2–3; Polletta 2003, 56–63; Ransby 2003, 240–44). 'The democratic idea [was] that an oppressed group, class or community had the right to determine the nature of the fight to end its oppression' (Ransby 2003, 300).

The constituent elements of this discourse rest on two key concepts: the construction of 'ordinary people' and the process of decision-making for collective action. Each of these concepts will be discussed in turn below. I think it is important to note at this stage, however, that the foundation of participatory democracy is the quality of the social relationships within the collective. By emphasising the process of creating and maintaining non-hierarchical and non-competitive social relations whereby authority is invested in the group rather than in any individual or dominant 'expert', it appears that the Democracy discourse is seeking to construct a moral identity that attempts to balance the processes and the outcomes of radical social change (Hayden 1961, 26; Polletta 2003, 122–3; Ransby 2003, 240–4).

Striving to achieve equality within local groups and throughout society requires a radical re-imagining of the 'community' in the Democracy discourse. The discourse shifts the traditional constructions of leaders and followers through a particular construction of 'indigenous leadership'. For radical social change to take place, ordinary people – those not traditionally considered appropriate, respectable or capable – had to be the leaders and strategists of community organisations. For example, here is Tom Hayden (1965 quoted in Polletta 2004, 72), one of the founders of Students for a Democratic Society (SDS), a radical white student organisation modelled on and heavily influenced by the work of SNCC, discussing the need for indigenous leadership:

> What will happen to America if the people who least 'qualify' for leadership begin to demand control over the decisions affecting their lives? The most thoroughly embedded if subtle quality of American life is its elitism – economic, political, social and psychological.

Thus the goals of community organising, and, by extension, the major social movements such as the Civil Rights Movement, had to be both building indigenous leadership and the dismantling of the structures that produced the social, political and economic inequality of African Americans and other marginalised groups. The Democracy discourse constructs the process of building a movement of people to articulate and demand social, political and economic rights as of equal importance as the success of achieving those rights: 'Whatever you seek to achieve as an end must be evidenced in the process by which you seek to accomplish it' (Polletta 2004, 61).

Building indigenous leadership requires not only a commitment to democratic ideals but also the adoption of a set of particular practices to support the decision-making and collective action of local people. Community groups require open and flexible organisational structures to support collective discussions and decision-making. The concept of 'group-centred leadership' rather than 'leader-centred groups' means that local movements need to be structured as pre-figurative spaces so that people can organise themselves for education and action (Baker 1960, 1; Ransby 2003, 27–4; Polletta 2004, 63–4). For the Democracy discourse, 'pre-figurative spaces' means modelling the social relations which produce the desired relationships in a future radical democratic society. 'There was certainly a pre-figurative, utopian dimension to participatory democracy as an organisational process [in SNCC], a sense that building a democratic movement in the here and now would lay the groundwork for a radically egalitarian society' (Polletta 2004, 205). Thus by eschewing unilateral decision-making and hierarchical leadership local people learn new ways of relating to each based on equality and respect. Through collective decision-making local people learn how to negotiate, strategise and be accountable to each other. By focusing on group consensus, leadership is invested in the collective rather than in any individual. Finally, the process of deliberation helps to build solidarity and sustain people's commitment to the movement. Here is Ella Baker (1972: 347), an early supporter and mentor of SNCC, discussing the importance of democratic spaces for developing leadership and agency: 'In the long run they themselves [local people] are the only protection they have against violence and injustice...People have to be made to understand that they cannot look for salvation anywhere but themselves'.

I will now move to discuss the identity constructions of the Democracy discourse. Because the structure of discourse is focused on building non-hierarchical and democratic spaces for deliberation and action, the discourse constitutes the identities of actors involved in the community organising process in a very interesting way. A key identity is the 'community organiser' whose role is to engage in an explicitly educational process with the indigenous leadership and support them in creating spaces for learning and action (Mueller 1993, 51–3; Carson 1995, 133). The Democracy discourse constructs community organisers not as leaders of local movements but facilitators who help build trust and solidarity between people and support people in their own self-directed process for social change. Community organisers 'had to suppress their own egos and personal organisational ambitions as much as possible and to approach local communities with deference and humility' (Ransby 2003, 274).

Thus the community organiser is not the focus within the Democracy discourse; the emphasis is on the *process* of building spaces whereby community organisers and indigenous leaders encounter each other based on equality and respect in order to take collective action:

> Creating a moral community within the movement was essential to making political change. Mutual trust, respect, equality...enabled organisers to build the leadership of the politically inexperienced and reinforced their own sense of organising. (Polletta 2004: 122–3)

The creation of a community organiser identity makes possible the facilitation of spaces for the practice of radical democracy and identifying and supporting indigenous leaders for their own self-directed process of social change. As Baker (1968 quoted in Payne 1989, 892) argues: 'I have always thought what is needed is the development of people who are not interested in being leaders as much as developing leadership among other people'.

The Democracy discourse also constructs an equal and complementary identity of 'local people' or 'indigenous leaders' for the community groups also involved in civil rights work. It is important to note that local people are constructed as deliberative and active agents in the struggle for equality and rights. This is, I argue, the distinguishing feature of the Democracy discourse and sets it apart from other community development discourses in both America and Britain over the next 40 years. For example, here are two examples from Lewis discussing the leadership and agency of local people:

> You don't have to wait until Roy Wilkins [the head of the NAACP] comes to Jackson [Mississippi]. You don't have wait until Martin Luther King comes to McComb [Georgia]. You can do it *yourself*. There is no one more powerful force than *you*. There is no leader as powerful as *you* if you pull together. (Lewis 1998, 188; emphasis in original text)

As we can see the focus in the discourse is on building the collective leadership and agency of local people:

> We were meeting people on their terms, not ours. If they were out in the field picking cotton, we would go in that field and pick with them…Before we ever got around to saying what we had to say, we listened. And in the process we build up both their trust in us and their confidence in themselves. (Lewis 1998 quoted in Ransby 2003: 282)

The goal of working with local people was to help '[develop] a sense of worth and leadership among people who had never been held in high regard in their communities' (Ransby 2003: 305). Importantly, however, through its emphasis on group-centred leadership the Democracy discourse seems to also be attempting to embed principles of equality and respect in its attendant identities that structures the organisers' relationship with local people. By constructing everyone as a leader, this discourse appears to be trying to subvert the hierarchy and elitism that typically constitute relations between organisers and activists. Again, here is Baker (1972, 352) reflecting and approving of this process:

> Every time I see a young person who has come through the system to a stage where he could profit from the system…

but who identifies more with the struggle of black people who have not had his chance…I take new hope.

Finally, Democracy discourse's identity constructions sharply contrast with other competing discourses at this time. Other civil rights organisations that produce and reproduce competing discourses are constructed as both hypocritical and ineffective. These organisations are represented as hypocritical because they only worked with and were staffed by middle-class elites; the voices and experiences of ordinary people were not represented in these organisations thus calling into question these organisations' claims for equality and justice. Here is a typical construction which is widely assumed to be an attack on the NAACP, the premier Black bourgeois organisation:

> Those who are well-heeled don't want to get un-well-heeled…If they are acceptable to the Establishment and they're wielding power which serves their interest, they can assume too readily that that also serves the interest of everybody. (Baker 1968 quoted in Ransby 2003, 305–6)

The Democracy discourse also constructs these rival organisations as ineffective because of their use of hierarchical structures and dependency on charismatic leadership. Supporting a charismatic leader is fundamentally anti-democratic and re-enforces the belief that only some people have the ability and capacity to be a leader. In a veiled attack on Martin Luther King Jr., and his organisation, the Southern Christian Leadership Conference (SCLC) Baker (1960, 1) states:

> [SNCC's] inclination toward group-centered leadership, rather than toward a leader-centered group pattern of organization, was refreshing indeed to those of the older group who bear the scars of the battle, the frustrations and the disillusionment that come when the prophetic leader turns out to have heavy feet of clay.

From 1960 to 1968 the Democracy discourse dominated constructions of identity within the Civil Rights Movement. To be sure, competing discourses did have influence, the most obvious being that associated with the texts and practices of the moderate and charismatic Martin Luther King Jr. As I previously discussed, however, by 1968 a key historical moment was unfolding to which the Democracy discourse was unable to respond effectively. With the goals of Black resistance shifting from civil rights to social and economic rights, the Democracy discourse was slowly marginalised.

This marginalisation was reinforced by the oral character of the discourse. I think that the strength of the Democracy discourse is its fluidity; its structure changes according to different contexts because its internal logic dictates that ordinary people have to define for themselves the terms of their struggle. Crucially, this discourse relied on oral traditions – its focus on dialogue and deliberation as both political education and the building of solidarity – in order to survive. The rise and subsequent domination of competing discourses during this time was helped by the strategic use of print media. This is not the case with the Democracy discourse. With the exception of Zinn (1964), promotional materials and retrospective interviews with activists and organisers, few substantial contemporary and popular texts exist which discuss in depth the Democracy discourse's ideas, concepts or practices. The direct voice of this discourse is only found in a specialist texts directly aimed at participants in SNCC; it is only through a recent and self-conscious reclaiming and compiling of data related to this discourse that the ideas, concepts and practices of the Democracy discourse is now better understood (for example see: Carson 1995; Lewis 1998; Polletta 2004; Ransby 2003; Payne 2007).

Thus in 1968 there was a blank textual space that other competing discourses could occupy and dominate with their own hegemonic interpretations of ideas and events. As a result, the Democracy discourse was silenced – written out of the history of community organising and development – by competing discourses. If it was mentioned at all – allusions are made to it in Carmichael and Hamilton (1967, 41–47) – it is constructed as well meaning but essentially misguided. In the other dominant text, the Democracy discourse is misrepresented as both nihilistic terrorism and the indulgences of the politically naïve (Alinsky 1971, xiv). I will discuss the misrepresentations of the Democracy discourse in further detail below.

These hegemonic misrepresentations of the Democracy discourse have profound implications for the discourses of community development and the identities mobilised within them. It appears that an entire tradition of ideas and practices has been marginalised and community development's ideas of radicalism are perhaps not fully informed by its own history. In my later chapters I will point out echoes and traces of the Democracy discourse; however, the discourse never regains dominance within later formations of community development. The way in which this discourse is marginalised during this moment in time matters because, as I shall demonstrate in later chapters, community development does not seem to be able construct identities derived from notions of equality and social justice. The marginalisation of the Democracy discourse perhaps helps to explain community development's gradual shift away from issues related to process (building consensus-based, non-hierarchical organisations) towards outcome-focussed work (setting and evaluating outputs, targets and deliverables). This will be discussed in more detail in Chapters Four and Six. The marginalisation of the Democracy discourse may also help to explain the pattern in the discourses of community development in which the idea of 'indigenous leaders' shifts over time from proactive subjects invested with agency to victims, dupes or those suffering from false consciousness requiring a leader or an expert to show them the path of enlightenment.

To fully understand the marginalisation of the Democracy discourse and the implications this has for community development, however, we must turn now to analyse the competing Power discourse.

## The rise and rise of the Power discourse

I have combined two seemingly contrasting political philosophies – Black Power and Alinskyism – into a single discursive category. Black Power, though a contested concept, is an ideology of Black self-determination through the establishment of norms, values, traditions and institutions that foster Black self-confidence, pride and self-sufficiency. Alinskyism is a form of community development focused on the zero-sum game of taking power from institutional elites for the benefit of community groups. To be sure, Saul Alinsky and Black Power activists did not share similar goals when they interacted with each other – especially in Chicago during the mid- to late 1960s. The ideas and practices of these two movements seemingly lead community development down different paths. Black Power and Alinskyism, however, share underlying patterns in language, social practices and identity constructions that continue to have important influences on community development identity and discourse today. What unites Black Power and Alinskyism, I argue, is the shift in language from democracy to zero-sum power plays and from idealism to real politick and with this shift in language comes a shift in identity: from a fluid and open community organiser identity to an exclusive 'vanguard' identity who dominates passive and misguided community groups.

I shall discuss each of the components of the Power discourse in turn. First, I will define the key components of Black Power and then analyse the identity constructions that Black Power constitutes. I will then turn to discuss the key concepts of Alinskyism and analyse those associated identity constructions.

Black Power comes to prominence due to four key events: the frustrations I outlined earlier in this chapter regarding the persistence of Black social and economic inequality; the perceived political and economic powerlessness of Black people in American society; a growing Black collective consciousness and racial pride in a positive 'Black' identity; and a backlash against the civil rights aims and practices (Carmichael and Hamilton 1967; Carson 1995; Polletta 2004). Here is Stokely Carmichael, the former Chairperson of SNCC (who deposed John Lewis in 1965) and an early adopter of the term 'Black Power' articulating the shift from civil rights to Black Power:

> We [civil rights activists] had nothing to offer that they [black people] could see, except to go out and be beaten again…For once, black people are going to use the words they want to use – not just the words whites want to hear. (Carmichael 1966 quoted in Carson 1995, 219)

For activists, Black Power is required to prevent the damaging effects of white social, political, economic and cultural hegemony over Black people:

> The social effects of colonialism are to degrade and dehumanise the subjected black man…White society maintains an attitude of superiority and the black community has too often succumbed to it…Racist assumptions of white superiority have been so deeply ingrained into the fibre of society that they infuse the entire functioning of the national subconscious. They are taken for granted and frequently not even recognized. (Carmichael and Hamilton 1967, 47)

Racism is defined in the discourse as both a socio-economic and psychological condition that causes and perpetuates Black inequality and powerlessness. In order to undermine and challenge the 'white power structure', what is required is the development of Black Power: 'the time is long overdue for the black community to redefine itself, set forth new values and goals and organise around them' (Carmichael and Hamilton 1967, 48). The ultimate focus of Black Power is the creation of new definitions of 'Blackness', understanding and reclaiming a silenced but distinctive heritage and tradition and identifying the self-interest of the 'Black community' in order to build alternative structures that promote the political and economic power of Blacks:

> Whites can only subvert our true search and struggles for self-determination, self-identification, and liberation in this country...Too long have we allowed white people to interpret the importance and meaning of the cultural aspects of our society. We have allowed them to tell us what was good about our Afro-American music, art, and literature... A thorough re-examination must be made by black people concerning the contributions that we have made in shaping this country. (SNCC 1968, 3)

The Power discourse's particular construction of self-determination is an important difference from the Democracy discourse. Self-determination as defined in the Democracy discourse was an empty signifier that local people could define for themselves. In the Power discourse, self-determination is linked to conquering the false consciousness of Black inferiority and the unnecessary and futile cooperation with whites for Black liberation. By subverting this false consciousness, ordinary Black people are able to develop racial pride and work towards seizing power from whites to build powerful all-Black institutions:

> The myth that the Negro is somehow incapable of liberating himself, is lazy...Negroes in this country have never been allowed to organise themselves because of white interference. As a result of this, the stereotype has been reinforced that blacks cannot organise themselves... If we are to proceed toward true liberation, we must cut ourselves off from white people. We must form our own institutions, credit unions, co-ops, political parties, write our own histories. (SNCC 1968, 1–2)

Thus, the focus in this discourse is the about over-throwing white hegemony and building a power base for Black people so they can exercise self-determination to achieve political and economic justice and equality. In order to achieve these new forms of power requires an embrace of a homogeneous, authentic and racialised identity of Blackness: a unified Black perspective for understanding the world and building solidarity among all Black people.

The Power discourse's emphasis on the concepts of 'power' and 'Blackness' has important implications for identity constructions. The central practice of the discourse is the construction of a Black revolutionary vanguard identity whose goal is to subvert white power and exhort Black people to develop an authentic revolutionary consciousness derived from Black Power principles. In opposition to the Democracy discourse, the vanguard identity in the Power discourse is not an organiser, facilitator nor a democratic educator. Instead, the vanguard is the leader of the masses of Black people. The goal of the vanguard is to: 'awaken...[and] educate the black community...to break open the chains in the minds of people' (SNCC 1966 quoted in Polletta 2003, 28).

In contrast to the Power discourse's construction of a Black revolutionary vanguard, it constructs two distinct and subordinate identities: the 'bewildered' Black community and the naïve 'radical'. The bewildered Black community is perhaps the most important identity construction in the Power discourse. The Black community is rendered an abstract and homogeneous mass that is misguided through false consciousness perpetuated by the white power structure. Unlike the Democracy discourse that constructs local people as leaders and agents, the Power discourse constructs Black people as passive objects devoid of agency who are to be acted on by revolutionary leaders. Here is the influential political scientist Reed (1986, 58–66) discussing this construction of the 'Black mass':

> The representation of the black community as a collective subject neatly concealed the system of hierarchy that mediated the relations between the leaders and the led... 'Community control' called not for direction of pertinent institutions...by their black constituents but for the administration of these institutions by alleged representatives in the name of the black community...Black control was by no means equivalent to popular democratisation.

Furthermore, Black people require development – not into leaders – but into a regimented form of 'authentic' Blackness so that they can then exercise some unspecified form of power. 'Most [Black Power activists] feel that black people must acquire black consciousness before they can successfully develop the tools and techniques for acquiring black power' (Ladner 1972 quoted in Robnett 1997, 179).

Interestingly, the Power discourse also misrepresents the competing Democracy discourse as naïve. In an important hegemonic practice, the

Power discourse reconstructs the Democracy discourse as ineffective, foolhardy and harmful to the self-interests of Black people. Here are two examples of misrepresenting the Democracy discourse as manipulative (because it does not work to promote Black Power) and as ridiculous (because of the emphasis on non-violence) from two early proponents of Black Power:

> I got out of that bag of manipulation…I went in there [Lowndes County where Carmichael help to found the first Black Panther Party] with certain ideas. One idea was to organise people to get power. If that's manipulation, so be it. (Carmichael 1966 quoted in Polletta 2003, 28)

> Now it is over. The days of singing freedom songs and combating bullets and billy clubs with love. They used to sing 'I Love Everybody'…now they sing: Too much love/ Too much love/Nothing kills a nigger like/Too much love.' (Lester 1966 quoted in Carson 1995, 237)

Through these types of misrepresentations, the Democracy discourse was marginalised by the Power discourse and Polletta (2003) attributes these types of antagonistic practices to contemporary claims that participatory democracy alienates minority ethnic groups and working class people through the imposition of a middle-class white culture onto social change organisations.

It is the notion of 'effectiveness' in practice and 'realism' in the analysis of the social relations that marks a key difference between the Power and Democracy discourses. The Power discourse as constructed in Alinskyism continues these discursive patterns. Alinskyism is most closely associated with the texts and practices of Saul Alinsky (1946; 1971) but extends beyond these writings to other followers in this tradition (Chambers 2003; Stoecker 2001; Bunyan 2010; Beck and Purcell 2013). Alinskyism is a self-proclaimed 'non-ideological' and populist approach to organising communities to build organisations capable of ascertaining collective self-interest by taking power from institutional decision-makers: 'We are concerned with how to create mass organisations to seize power and give it to the people. We are talking about a mass power organisation' (Alinsky 1971, 3).

To build a mass organisation, to be a 'realistic radical', requires an unsentimental understanding of the world: 'As an organiser I start from where the world is…not as I would like it to be; (Alinsky 1971, xix). The world is a place of 'power politics moved primarily by perceived immediate self-interests, where morality is rhetorical rationale for expedient action and self-interest' (Alinsky 1971, 13). Thus to spark radical changes requires mass organisations willing to muck in to this morass of conflicting interests in order to dominate proceedings to win power and influence for community groups.

Like the Black Power discourse, Alinskyism is using elitist language and constructing identities that allow for the domination of a 'realistic radical' and the subordination of a misguided and 'bewildered community'. This realistic radical has one populist belief that orientates his[6] actions: 'If the people have the power to act, in the long run they will, most of the time, reach the right decisions' (Alinsky 1971, 11–12). This radical is also a sage, however. Young people 'have no illusions about the system but plenty of illusions about the way to change our world. It is to this point that I have written this book' (Alinsky 1971, xiii). This elite construction of the realistic radical, similar to constructions of the revolutionary vanguard figure in Black Power, also undertakes a similar process of creating a subordinated identity for 'the people' and misrepresenting the Democracy discourse.

As in Black Power, the 'people' as constructed in Alinskyism are passive objects to be acted on by an enlightened radical organiser who sees the world clearly and who has the ability to build a power-based organisation. The people are thus described as:

> chained together by the common misery of poverty...
> ignorance, political impotence and despair... They are a mass
> of cold ashes of resignation and fatalism but inside there
> are glowing embers of hope which can be fanned by the
> building of means of obtaining power. (Alinsky 1971, 18–19)

It is the job of the radical organiser to lead people out of ignorance in order to gain power to exercise self-interest. Unchaining people from misery is difficult, however, and requires:

> a passive, affirmative, non-challenging attitude toward
> change among the mass of our people. They must feel...
> so defeated, so lost, so futureless in the prevailing system
> that they are willing to let go of the past and change their
> future. (Alinsky 1971, xix)

---

[6]    As will be discussed in greater detail in Chapter Four, the consequences of an Alinskyist discourse are the marginalisations of feminist and anti-racist philosophies and the male gendering of the community organiser identity.

This view of 'the people' is deeply problematic because it appears to undermine the Power discourse's commitment to building power for the powerless. This discourse constructs the people acting based on their self-interest, however, it does not seem possible for a passive object, as constructed above, to possess the ability or the capacity for agency. Because 'the people' are constructed as passive and ignorant, then the role of the radical organiser must be constructed as a dominant subject leading the people towards enlightenment and power. Indeed, this identity construction may help to explain why later texts which inherit some of the language and practices of the Power discourse devote so much space explaining the techniques of community organising rather than trying to understand the context and conflicting identities of community groups (for a further discussion of this point see Chapters Four and Six).

Like Black Power, Alinskyism also misrepresents the Democracy discourse in order to gain dominance. Consequently, the ideas and practices of the Democracy discourse have been constructed as both dangerous and naïve within the Power discourse. For example, in an allusion to Students for a Democratic Society disintegrating into the Weather Underground and former SNCC activists implicated in domestic terrorism, here is Saul Alinsky (1971: xiv–xviii) mocking the decline of participatory democracy:

> The young have seen their 'activist' participatory democracy turn into its antithesis – nihilistic bombing and murder… There are no rules for revolution…but there are rules for radicals…to know these is basic to a pragmatic attack on the system. These rules make the difference between being a realistic radical and being a rhetorical one who uses tired old words and slogans.

From the quote above it seems that until young radicals give up on the idea of pre-figurative spaces, being a band of brothers and living the values they believe in, they risk becoming ineffectual demagogues. This marginalisation of the Democracy discourse is an important development in the changing discourses and identities of community development since 1968. Community development's construction of 'radicalism' can be seen as misguided. Radicalism, as defined by the Power discourse, is the action of an elite few who dispense wisdom to the benighted mass of people suffering from false consciousness and complacency. Importantly, the goals of this radicalism remain undefined. In the Power discourse, radicalism is as abstract as building alternative institutions or people seizing power. How these ideas are defined, how groups might work to achieve these goals and what society would look like if power was redistributed or new institutions were created remains unclear. What is known is that the people may gain freedom from illusions about themselves and their society. The Democracy discourse's attempts to build democratic social relationships between individuals involved in struggle appear to have been lost. This alternative perspective on the meaning of 'radicalism', I argue, has been written out of the history of community development.

Helping to write the Democracy discourse out of the history of community development is the Poverty discourse. This relatively conservative discourse differs significantly from the two I analysed above but what the Poverty and Power discourses share are similar identity constructions and I will now turn to analyse the Poverty discourse in detail.

## The rise of technocracy and the Poverty discourse

> People were poor because they lacked political power, and the ways for them to escape poverty was to get political power – through the War on Poverty…The best instrument at hand for achieving this goal was the community action programme, and the best way to ensure that community action would be a means of empowerment for the poor was to the guarantee poor people 'maximum feasible participation' in the local community action agencies. (Lemann 1995, 151)

Unlike the anti-establishment Democracy and Power discourses, the Poverty discourse is constituted by the texts, language and practices of institutional actors wielding official state power. The Poverty discourse is constructed at the same moment as the Democracy discourse (it predates the Power discourse) and is constituted by the same issues of persistent African American poverty and inequality. Instead of interpreting Black social and economic inequality as the effect of institutionalised discrimination, however, the Poverty discourse constructs inequality to be the result of a failure of democratic institutions (public services such as education, housing and employment training) to be responsive to the needs of marginalised groups. Thus the discursive practices of the Poverty discourse are focused on coordinating institutional services through rational scientific planning and community consultation and participation. The Poverty discourse constructs the idea of 'community action' as:

> concerned above all with the reorganisation of local social services into an integrated plan to attack the roots of social deprivation. It was to be at once responsive to the people it served, imaginative and adaptive, comprehensively coordinated, informed by a systematic analysis of the causes of deprivation and methodically evaluated. (Marris and Rein 1972: 10)

In an important divergence from both the Democracy and Power discourses, 'community action' is constructed in the Poverty discourse as reform of democratic institutions as well as a transformation of the norms, values and culture of people living in poverty. The concept of 'reform' is a central idea in the Poverty discourse because it strikes at the heart of the way the discourse constructs reality:

> From the first, this movement of reform was concerned with poverty, it arose less from protest or moral indignation at injustice than from a sense of breakdown in the institutions which should be diffusing opportunities for all (Marris and Rein 1972, 23)

Unresponsive state institutions are not constructed as manifestations of white middle class values and power, but instead the welfare state is constructed as uncoordinated and bureaucratic. One of the causes of poverty is the breakdown of communication between different social welfare services, such as education and housing, and the reliance on outdated practices that are aided by a hierarchical bureaucratic culture of the state. Thus one major goal of reform was to 'alter the opportunity structure in education, employment [and] housing' (Marris and Rein 1972, 63). By promoting joint planning between different social services, by promoting poor people's participation in institutional decision-making and by creating alternative agencies armed with new ideas which were to be 'ruthlessly evaluated', reform could fulfil the promise of the American dream for the poor.

The Poverty discourse, however, constructs reform as also pertaining to the culture of people living in poverty. While avoiding the Victorian language of the undeserving poor, the Poverty discourse, however, does construct poor people as perpetuating a dysfunctional cycle of poverty that undermines any existing opportunities. The cycle of poverty – a lack of opportunities promoting alienation and delinquent behaviour and this behaviour limiting available opportunities – could be tackled by institutions expanding opportunities and by poor people eschewing delinquent behaviour and becoming responsible citizens through participation in institutional decision-making about their needs and interests.

In this discourse, with reform required for democratic institutions to perform more effectively and for the poor to help themselves by being responsible citizens, clear identities are constructed. Marris and Rein (1972, 29) articulate the construction of the 'reformer' identity in this way:

> A reformer in American society faces three crucial tasks. He must recruit a coalition of power sufficient for his purpose; he must respect the democratic tradition which expects every citizen not merely to be represented but to play an autonomous part in the determination of his own affairs and his policies must be rational.

The reformer in the Poverty discourse is a professional who uses expert knowledge to make rational decisions about anti-poverty work. Armed with scientific analyses about the causes of poverty, the reformer uses this exclusive knowledge to create and evaluate planned programmes that will address both the causes and effects of deprivation.

> We believe that an important characteristic which distinguishes the professional from the non-professional is his ability to utilise knowledge and theory in his work. (Brager and Specht 1973, vii)

Like the vanguard and the radical in the Power discourse, the rational reformer is also an elitist category that is invested with agency and this has problematic implications for constructions of community groups. While the rational reformer is a democrat who wishes to foster community participation in social welfare service planning and delivery, community groups in this discourse have been constructed as alienated and delinquent and this construction creates a paradox at the heart of the Poverty discourse.

On the one hand the poor are a 'leaderless, ill-educated and dispirited people' (Marris and Rein 1972, 213) and 'apathetic, inarticulate, incapable of formulating demands, or assisting and diagnosing their own needs' (Shriver 1966 quoted in Marris and Rein 1972, 90). The poor are constructed as passive and bewildered objects lacking agency. On the other hand, however, the poor are also defined as citizens with a potential for agency to run their own affairs, hence the focus on 'maximum feasible participation' of the poor in service planning and delivery. 'Nothing should be done for people that is not done with them...A mandate from established power does not excuse [the reformer] from securing the endorsement and participation of the people themselves' (Marris and Rein 1972, 31). As I have previously argued, the problem here is in how individuals and groups constructed as passive and ignorant objects have the capacity to deliberate and negotiate with the expert professional. By constructing the poor in this way, the discourse is unable to reconcile its secondary construction of the poor as a responsible citizen. As I demonstrated in the Power discourse, by positioning the poor as passive, this enhances the role of the reformer and ensures the professional will always act on the incorrigible poor.

Indeed this contradictory construction of the poor has real material consequences for discursive practices, as a New York City based community action project, Mobilisation for Youth, found when trying to promote participation in its decision-making structures. Because the poor where constructed as ill-educated, the organisation was sceptical of the participation of any intelligent and articulate poor people as they could not be the 'authentic' representation of the poor or reflect the 'real' interests of this group. Thus they focused their outreach work on those whom they deemed to be less intelligent and inarticulate to participate in decision-making. In response to this seemingly contradictory policy, a staffer in the Johnson Administration, Daniel Patrick Moynihan, who would go on to become an influential Senator, replied:

> Mobilisation for Youth is going to get hold of a lower level of true and genuine leaders who are − what? − inarticulate, irresponsible and relatively unsuccessful? I am sorry but I suspect that proposition...These are not the principles [to recruit] indigenous leadership. (Moynihan 1965 quoted in Marris and Rein 1972, 214−5)

As in the Power discourse, because the poor have been constructed as a passive and impotent object, the reformer must be invested with a dominant role, thus rendering the democratic possibilities for action difficult to attain. While it seems rational to look beyond working with community elites, if ordinary people are constructed as hapless delinquents, then it is irrational to support their participation, in spite of any democratic impulses.

## Conclusions

1968 can be understood as a moment of transition when the politics of the Civil Rights Movement were moving out of fashion and were being replaced by violent rebellion, a growing disillusionment with state institutions and new forms of technocratic politics. This period of transition also appears to influence the formation, structure and operation of the three community development discourses I identified in this chapter. I argued that rather than community development being infused by democratic egalitarian politics, it is dominated by two discourses – Power and Poverty – that on the surface seem different but ultimately construct community development processes and identities in similar ways. The construction of a revolutionary vanguard, a realistic radical or a rational reformer appears to require the construction of local people as passive, ignorant and incorrigible. In order to sustain the construction of the community development organiser or technocrat as a subject with a vision, rules, or rationality necessitates the construction of local people who are the opposite: who are blind, ill-disciplined or irrational. In doing so, it seems that American community development creates a perpetual justification for the domination and misrepresentation of community groups. Exploring how these broad debates about justice and equality play out in the narrow spaces of community development highlights the contradictory and perhaps unexpected micropolitics at play. As I shall demonstrate, these dilemmas of language and identity constructions in community development discourses are reproduced over a 40-year period in the American context.

Alternative approaches to community development as articulated in the Democracy discourse have been marginalised through both the changing political fortunes of the Civil Rights Movement and the hegemonic practices of rival discourses during this moment in time. As a result, important approaches to the construction of identity have been silenced in the community development discursive repertoire. As I shall demonstrate in subsequent chapters, the Democracy discourse's ideas of finding and developing indigenous leadership; building community organisations as pre-figurative spaces; and then taking seriously the process of consensus-based decision-making, remain stubbornly marginal ideas in the intellectual and activist traditions of community development in the United States. The opportunity for community development to provide an alternative to existing political and policy debates and practices is compromised because the dominant identity constructions during this moment appear to perpetuate rather than subvert inequality, hierarchy and elitism.

# CHAPTER THREE

# When technocracy met Marxism: community development projects in Britain

## Introduction

In the last chapter I discussed the formation and structure of three American community development discourses dating from 1968 to 1975. I demonstrated how, in the context of the problematic protest transition from civil rights to economic rights, the language and social practices of the once influential Civil Rights Movement fell out of favour. Filling the vacuum were two discourses – one focusing on zero-sum power plays and the other on rational scientific planning – both of which positioned community development as a hierarchical process of a professional or radical activist acting on a bewildered and confused community. In this chapter I will analyse the competing discourses and identities within the Urban Programme's Community Development Projects (CDPs) in Britain from 1968 to 1975. Unlike community development in the United States, and as I shall demonstrate in this chapter, community development in the UK should be understood primarily as an official institutional practice of the welfare state. From my analysis of texts I will show that community development is typically defined as a contentious state-sponsored activity whereby the goals and purposes of community development are contested between technocrats wielding official state power and some 'radical' community development professionals seeking to redistribute state power to local people.

I have identified two discourses for analysis in this chapter. The 'Rationalist discourse' is constituted by the texts, language and practices of the Wilson Government's Home Office and the Gulbenkian Foundation which sought to construct and prescribe a framework for a new emerging profession called 'community work' to support the efficient coordination of local government service delivery and counter a destructive 'pathology of the poor'. The 'Structuralist discourse' is constituted by the texts, language and practices of those newly created professional community workers seeking to reconstruct the identity and practices of both the community development profession and the role of the state in order to support the redistribution of power, wealth and resources to working class communities. Although the discursive repertoires of the Structuralist and Rationalist discourses appear to be in conflict, I shall demonstrate that there are few significant differences between these two discourses. Although the role of the state and the professional is contested between these two discourses, what remains uncontested in each of the discourses is that the state and the professional – not local people – are constructed as the key subjects invested with agency and the central agents to achieve social change.

I will begin this chapter by first putting the 1968–1975 moment into a distinctive British context. Similar to the United States, this is also a transitional moment in the UK; it is constructed as a time of rapid technological, economic and social change whereby 'less resilient' people require support to reconcile themselves to new ways of living and being. The peculiar way in which this moment in time is constructed is significant because the definition of both problems and solutions during this transformative moment in British community development is macro-focussed. As a consequence, it is the state, rather than local people, that is the active subject within British community development discourses at this time.

## The welfare state and social change

> Western social democracy has learnt much about ways of making available to majority groups the benefits of science and technology. It is now urgent – ethically, socially and politically – to do the same for minority groups, and especially for those suffering many inter-related problems and deprivations. This is partly a technical and administrative problem. (CDA 1968 quoted in Loney 1983, 48)

1968 is a politically salient moment in time in Britain because of the emergence of two inter-related issues: a popular perception that rapid social, economic and technological changes were afoot and a simultaneous call for a technical reform of the state (Hill 1970; Miliband 1973; Hain 1976; Cockburn 1977). From the slum clearances in the inner-cities and the relocation of residents to peripheral housing estates; to an increase in immigration from the Commonwealth and the white working-class backlash as encapsulated in Enoch Powell's *Rivers of Blood* speech; to the growing automation in the manufacturing and heavy industries and the resulting rise in unemployment, 'social change' was affecting many facets of British life (Calouste Gulbenkian Foundation 1968, 9–14; 1973; CDP 1977, 3–5; Loney 1983, 8–16). The multifaceted nature of social change was defined by key authors of this time as a macro-level process by which global social and economic forces were transforming traditional ways of life. Importantly, the welfare state was defined as an important player in helping ordinary people reconcile themselves to the depth, breadth and rapidity of this change:

> A consequence of the speed of change is that many people are jerked out of one way of life into another perhaps more demanding, and at any rate, unfamiliar [life]…Most people are sufficiently socialised and self-reliant [but expertise is needed] to help people and the providers of services to bring about a more comfortable 'fit' between themselves and constant change. (Calouste Gulbenkian Foundation 1968, 28–9)

This understanding of social change and the solutions offered to ameliorate its effects is crucial to understanding how the discourses of British community development respond to this politically salient moment. For community development, this moment in time is not, perhaps surprisingly, linked to rebellion against social hierarchies, unjust war or new forms of democracy as seen in the protest movements in the United States. I do not mean to suggest that social movements – most notably the feminist, student and anti-war movements – were absent and did not influence profoundly influence community development. Rather, what I wish to highlight as distinctive about the micropolitics of British community development at this moment are the struggles about the meaning and purpose of the welfare state in the lives of ordinary people:

> More than ever before, men now live in the shadow of the state. What they want to achieve, individually or in groups, now mainly depends on the state's sanction and support… It is for the state's attention, or for its control, that men compete; and it is against the state that beat the waves of social conflict. (Miliband 1969, 8)

Unlike America where the state is viewed with deep suspicion and from which community development does not take its primary orientation, it is important to note that the state is the *key protagonist* in British community development. Given the very different histories of welfare state formation in America and Britain, this is not surprising. Nevertheless, the tradition of social democracy and the assumption of the active role the state should play in the lives of British citizens has profound implications for the ways in which British community development generates its particular ideas and social practices.

Thus state actors respond to this particular understanding of the problem of change by seeking to reform aspects of the welfare state by implementing rational and technical decision-making processes to address social problems (Titmuss 1968; Greaves 1976; Loney 1983; Jones 2006). This 'professionalisation of reform' would replace capricious and expedient policy decisions and would instead use the expert power of research and evaluation in order to make evidence-based and objective decisions regarding solutions to social problems. Here is the Calouste Gulbenkian Foundation (1968, 12–14) praising this new technocratic response to social change:

> The change in the role of government from the regulative to the dynamic has produced...positive social policy interventions...The participation of social scientists and social workers in planning is necessary so that the human consequences of technological change may be given their proper weight together with physical and economic consequences.

Decision-making by the state during this moment 'reflect[s] both the concern with more efficient resource development and the commitment to a greater role for social science in the development of social policy' (Loney 1983, 16). Thus what we see emerge at this time is a renewed 'activist' state armoured with the social research in order to facilitate policy development and implementation. In this context, the emerging community development profession is from the beginning placed in a space of hierarchical, rational and scientific practices seemingly divorced from the everyday experiences of local people. The texts which constitute the Rationalist discourse are drawn from these technocratic responses to social change (Calouste Gulbenkian Foundation 1968; Loney 1983).

During this moment, however, the nature and purpose of this activist state is contested. Socialist academics, activists and policy makers, disillusioned with Wilson's Labour government, were also concerned with the rapidity of social change in terms of the transformation of capital and the impact this was having on working class communities. The welfare state, in terms of its bureaucratic structures and resource allocation, was identified as a new and important location for class struggle:

> We have to recognise that alongside struggle at the point of production, in the mines and factories, there is a struggle at the point of reproduction, in schools, on housing estates, in the street, in the family…Struggles around housing or benefits or schools are economic…Those things too must be protected against the…pressure of profit. (Cockburn 1977, 163)

Because public services, such as housing, education and health, generate and reproduce particular relationships between citizens and the state, socialists, academics and activists define state structures as an important and legitimate site of protest and political struggle alongside the traditional sphere of the workplace. Socialists argued that the state – rather than being a neutral actor addressing social problems – was actually an apparatus used by the capitalist class to wield power. In order to build a democratic socialist state capable of redistributing wealth and power, the existing state apparatus had to be dismantled. Here is Ralph Miliband (1973, 32) in his influential articulation of this perspective:

> In the Marxist scheme, the 'ruling class' of capitalist society is that class which owns and controls the means of production and which is able, by virtue of economic power thus conferred upon it, to use the state as its instrument for the domination of society.

The state, rather than being a champion of social reform, could in fact simply further the interests of a powerful elite. Thus, political action in relation to the state was in constant danger of cooptation. As Peter Hain (1976, 17) argues: 'the fact that many groups have been absorbed as appendages to the welfare state, rather than alternatives to it, can be explained partly by the absence of a clear theory of social change through community action'. Texts which constitute the Structuralist discourse are drawn from these sceptical socialist analyses about the ability of the state to advance social justice (Baine 1974; Dearlove 1974; ELCU 1974; Mayo 1977; CDP 1977; CDP 1978).

I think it is nonetheless important to highlight the unintentional consensus between the rational social planners and the socialist sceptics of the welfare state. Because these two groups identify similar social problems to be tackled and attribute these problems to macro-level social and economic processes, they end up reaching similar conclusions about the agents of social change. By attributing disruptive social changes to British life to state failure, capitalist development and poor decision-making by politicians and policy makers, the actions of ordinary people appear to be marginalised and downplayed during this moment in time. Instead, the agents of change are assumed to be the state and state actors. Throughout this chapter I will be highlighting the overlooked consensus about the agency of the state between technocrats and the 'radical' professionals. In the context of community development, this interpretation of agency is very important. As I shall also demonstrate in this chapter, because community development is created and practiced in institutional spaces, this appears to define community development in such a way as to downplay or ignore the experiences, perceptions, contributions and actions of ordinary people in transforming their lives.

With this context of 1968 as a backdrop – social problems and solutions defined and potentially resolved in the context of the state and macro-level processes – I will now analyse the micropolitics of the competing community development discourses and identity constructions during this moment.

## The Rationalist discourse and the activist state

The Rationalist discourse is constituted by the texts, language and practices of the Home Office under the Wilson Government, which was seeking to restructure the welfare state and the Gulbenkian Foundation, which was tasked by the Wilson Government with inventing a new profession to support the Government's planned institutional reforms. The Urban Programme was initiated by Harold Wilson's government in order to:

> find out how to give cooperation between services a more
> solid foundation...Familiar activities need to be conducted
> in new ways in order to make services more accessible and
> comprehensible to those who will not otherwise see them
> as relevant...More fundamentally, the project must seek to
> involve the people living in the area in community schemes.
> (CDA 1968 quoted in Loney 1983, 2–3)

Modelled on the American War on Poverty programme as discussed in Chapter Two, the assumption driving the Urban Programme was that poverty persisted among specific groups due to the poor coordination of local government service delivery combined with a social pathology which afflicted people living in poverty. The Community Development Project (CDP) was the flagship initiative of the Urban Programme which sought to use expert-driven research to better understand poverty and inequality which would lead to the more efficient organisation of social services which would in turn engender resilience and self-help among the poor (Calouste Gulbenkian Foundation 1968, 1973; Loney 1983; Jones 2006). Unlike the American War on Poverty, the participation of the poor in the decision-making of the state was not an explicit objective of the CDP – ensuring that the poor used services more effectively thus making poor people more self-reliant and relieving pressure on local services was the goal (Calouste Gulbenkian Foundation 1968, 1973, 3–5; Loney 1983, 2–3).

Twelve projects were set up across the UK between 1970–71 to operate for five years to coordinate local services in Coventry, Liverpool, Glamorgan, Southwark, Batley, Newham, Paisley, Cumberland, Newcastle, Birmingham, Oldham and Tyneside (Calouste Gulbenkian Foundation 1968, 1973; CDP 1977; Loney 1983; Jones 2006). The dominant narrative in the early years of the projects was the promotion of consensual partnership-working between service providers in health, education, housing and employment in order to make their services more accessible and holistic for people in poverty:

> The existing services are vertically organised. In varying degrees each exists to meet a particular need or a range of needs, the assumption being that other needs will be met by the clients themselves or by the other services...[People in poverty] need support from the social services which is not offered piecemeal...but which can help them face these problems as a whole. (CDA 1968 quoted in Loney 1983, 53–4)

Cooperative working would help local government to 'discover and develop methods of helping the severely deprived to make a personally constructive use of the social services' (CDP 1969 quoted in Loney 1983, 55). I think it is important to note at this stage how the focus of attention of the CDP and hence the professionals employed by it is on the state. The Rationalist discourse constructs the state as a key subject invested with agency to resolve the problems of people living in poverty. As a result, the state and its agents are the active subjects while people living in poverty are to be acted on by these cooperating and consensual experts: 'The prime objective of Government was to maximise the total supply of welfare...and second to produce a more equitable distribution of welfare' (Home Office 1969, quoted in Loney 1983, 56).

In an important hegemonic practice, the Rationalist discourse constructs a new type of professional to support the cooperation and trust between service providers. The new community development professional is constructed as a public administrator whose job is to be a 'change agent' both within local government and within poor communities. This administrator finds innovative ways to break down bureaucracy and departmentalism in local government that cause inefficiencies in service planning and delivery. This new professional is also a catalyst for change within deprived areas because by 'understanding the relationship of man to his environment and to his fellow man' the professional can help reconcile people to the bewildering changes in their daily lives (Calouste Gulbenkian Foundation 1968, 28). Reconciling people to social change involves building a sense of community and engaged citizenship among marginalised groups in order to understand and try to resolve individual and collective needs:

> There is a more active function [of the work of the community development professional] in stimulating people to meet some local need and trying to identify the leaders in a neighbourhood who could with support carry other people along with them. (Calouste Gulbenkian Foundation 1968, 29)

The construction of the community development professional as a 'technical man' who uses 'social philosophy, psychology and sociology as well as geography and economics' to facilitate social reform allows for a dominant role of the state and the expert and marginalises and subordinates community groups (Calouste Gulbenkian Foundation 1968, 28). For example, civil servants setting out the ultimate goal of the CDP describe it as such:

> It is already known that the symptoms of personal, family and community malfunctioning can be diminished by increasing the level of external support...The end [of the CDPs] will be to discover and demonstrate new methods of reaching a minority of the population suffering from

> multi-deprivation and of enabling them to function more autonomously. (CDA 1968 quoted in Loney 1983, 50)

It is important to note how the identity of the community development professional is unclear within the Rationalist discourse, however. Although the profession's goal is to reform local services and the character of poor people, the identity of this professional is muddled. The Calouste Gulbenkian Foundation's (1968, 1973) hegemonic texts on community development demonstrate the contingency of the identity of the professional. The Foundation in some places states that community development workers should be mid-career professionals in education and health, while in other places stating that community development workers should be change agents promoting democratic participation and in other places that community development workers should be senior civil servants interested in professional development. The Foundation (1968, 3) debates whether workers should be deployed in 'new or deprived neighbourhoods or with underprivileged or deviant groups…[or whether the professional should train] other professionals, administrators, planners…about community needs and processes and the importance of associating the consumers in the planning and operation of services'. Ultimately, the Foundation settles on this half-way house construction of the profession: 'community work…is a function which is or should be exercised by many different people as part of their professional activities or as voluntary workers' (Calouste Gulbenkian Foundation 1968, 27).

In other words, a community development worker can be anyone either inside or outside the state seemingly doing anything at the grassroots level. This ambiguity regarding the identity of the community development professional is important as it helps to explain the repetitions, patterns and preoccupations in the Rationalist discourse regarding the identity of the community development worker. The preoccupation with constructing and reconstructing community development workers' identity may well help to explain why so little attention focuses on the construction of local people and why local people are marginalised in key British community development texts during this politically salient moment.

Unsurprisingly then, this ambiguous and contingent community development professional is engaged in a seemingly baffling and contradictory array of practices constructed as 'community development':

> [Community development is] part of a protest against apathy
> and complacency against distant and anonymous authority.
> It is also part of the whole dilemma of how to reconcile
> the 'revolution of human dissent' into the large-scale
> organisation and economic and social planning…This boils
> down to how to give meaning to democracy…The question
> for community workers is whether organisational structures
> can be devised and people trained and employed to facilitate
> citizen participation and to make it more effective, as well
> as making public and voluntary services more acceptable
> and usable. In short, community work is a means of giving
> life to local democracy. (Calouste Gulbenkian Foundation
> 1968, 5)

That community development is constructed as the process of giving
meaning to democracy but that democracy appears tied to the structure
of the welfare state is problematic. High quality public service provision
is a crucial element of social citizenship and forms an important part
of making democracy meaningful for different groups. Democracy,
however, is not solely a function of the state nor does the practice of
democracy necessarily have to take place in state-sponsored spaces.
Again, because the rationalist welfare state is the key subject within
British community development it appears to dominate and silence
alternative identities for community development professionals and
alternative constructions about the nature and practice of democracy
during this moment.

The implications for identity construction within the Rationalist
discourse are clear. There are two dominant identities with an uneasy
relationship with each other and this relationship helps to marginalise
local people in this discourse. One identity is the activist welfare state.
The mechanics of the structure of the state – the coordination of local
service provision – dominate this discourse. For example:

> [One of the aims of community work is] the democratic
> process of involving people in thinking, deciding, planning
> and playing an active part in the development and operation
> of services that affect their daily lives. (Calouste Gulbenkian
> Foundation 1968, 4)

Allied to this identity is the ambiguous community development
professional, which I discussed above, tasked with administrating
changes in state structures and in doing so facilitating self-help among

the poor. 'Many councils have been very uncertain as to what these community workers should actually do, and the task of their new employees has often been to define their own jobs' (Hain 1976, 18). This fractured identity of the community development professional may be why so little space is devoted to constructing equal and just identities for local people. Very few constructions of local people exist and those that do reflect the domination of these two identities and the subordination of local people to these identities. Local people are constructed in various ways as passive and/or depoliticised objects:

> A community development officer is recommended as a way of communicating with the majority of 'passive' members of the community who do not belong to local groups... It is very hard to help the less articulate members of the community to express their ideas and take action upon them. (Hill 1970, 215)

The Calouste Gulbenkian Foundation (1968, 9–11) alternates its description of community groups as: 'consumers of services', 'underprivileged', 'deviant' or 'depressed minorities'. The overarching construction of local people, however, is that of being besieged and overwhelmed by the rapidity of macro-level changes and being incapable of responding effectively to these changes. For example:

> The demand that those who use services should have a say in their operation is often nullified by growth in size and complexity which makes it less and less possible for the man in the street to exercise an informed judgement about such matters... To press people to assume responsibilities beyond their powers creates disillusionment; but it is essential that they should exercise these capacities up to the limit if local democracy is to have meaning. (Calouste Gulbenkian Foundation 1968, 14)

This construction is perhaps not surprising given the assumption within the Rationalist discourse that the poor suffer from a destructive pathology of delinquency and family breakdown which traps them in poverty. It is noteworthy that for a social process to both coordinate service delivery and to build poor people's self-reliance, however, the Rationalist's construction of community development appears to have very little to do with understanding social relationships, culture and democracy at the local level and seems to be in fact focused solely on improved public administration. Indeed, as the Calouste Gulbenkian Foundation (1968, 3) argues: '[community work is needed because] discovering how to bring about small and psychological change among groups of people in a locality is (or should be) a precondition of planned physical change'.

Perhaps the Rationalist discourse's identity constructions and discursive practices are not surprising given that this is the official discourse of the British state in 1968. What makes the micropolitics of British community development distinctive, however, is that the oppositional Structuralist discourse does not seem to challenge these elitist assumptions about professionalism, expertise or the role of the state in people's lives.

I will now move on to discuss the Structuralist discourse in further detail.

## The Structuralist discourse and the activist state

> [A new generation of activists] saw behind the façade of 'rights' and 'entitlements' and they began to point out that the welfare state was never intended to fulfil the function ascribed to it in popular mythology...The welfare state was a fraud and a 'con' and a very cheap buy for the ruling class. (East London Claimants Union 1974, 79)

The Structuralist discourse is constituted by the texts, language and practices of the newly created professionals and the community groups with whom they worked as part of the CDP. Like the Rationalist discourse, the Structuralist discourse is focused on the nature and structure of the state and to a lesser extent the construction of the professional working within institutional structures. It is important to note that the Structuralist discourse is *an evolution* of the Rationalist discourse within the CDP. By 1971, the dominant discourse with the CDP began to shift from Rationalist to Structuralist as community development professionals entered the field and began researching the nature of poverty and inequality in the twelve prescribed areas across Britain: 'A few months' field-work in areas suffering from long-term economic decline...was enough to provoke the first teams of CDP workers to question the Home Office's original assumptions' (CDP 1978, 4).

In a significant divergence, instead of interpreting the cause of poverty as the poor coordination of services or as a result of delinquency among people experiencing poverty, these new professionals located the cause of poverty and inequality in the operation of capitalism. Here are two examples of CDP workers providing an alternative explanation of poverty:

> There might certainly be in these areas a higher proportion of the sick and elderly for whom a better coordination of services would undoubtedly be helpful, but the vast majority were ordinary working-class men and women who, through forces outside their control, happened to be living in areas where bad housing conditions, redundancies, lay-offs and low-wages were common-place. (CDP 1978, 4)

> It became clear that the problems of these areas were firmly tied to much more basic structural problems in society... [There is a] recognition that the existence of such 'pockets of deprivation' is useful and even necessary to the normal operations of the economy, that capitalist development will always tend to produce such areas and the solution... is inextricably bound up with the critical problems of the British economy as a whole. (CDP 1977, 5)

Thus in my analysis of the Structuralist discourse it seems that understanding the nature of capitalism, the effects of capitalist underdevelopment on the psychology and agency of the working-class becomes the new dominant discourse and practice within the CDP. It is interesting to note the weak response of the Rationalist discourse to its successful marginalisation by the Structuralist discourse – the Home Office responded by simply ignoring the CDP. The Home Office continued supporting the CDP until the end of its funding cycle in 1975 and the Gulbenkian Foundation does not mention these developments at all. Loney (1983, 113) and Jones (2006, 157–8) argue that the Home Office lost interest in the CDP for two reasons. A key advocate of the initiative within the civil service, Derrick Morrell, died suddenly during the initial implementation of the project and as a result, interest in and enthusiasm for the CDP steadily declined within central government. In addition, the Wilson and Heath governments were distracted by more pressing concerns such as ongoing industrial disputes and the OPEC oil embargo that further eroded interest in the project. Tellingly, while this lack of interest in the CDP creates an opportunity for an oppositional discourse to develop it also means that the Structuralist discourse is constructed within a context of a wider marginalisation within central government thus rendering its ideas and practices less effective in influencing and shaping state structures and actors.

A key pattern in the language of the Structuralist discourse is the nature and structure of the state. Heavily influenced by Marx (1985), Gramsci (1984) and Althusser (1970) this discourse focuses on the multi-faceted domination and oppression of the working classes by state capitalism. Interpellating Marx, the Structuralist discourse first locates working class oppression in the history of industrial development in Britain (for a detailed discussion of this see: CDP 1977). Because Britain was the first industrialised nation, the British working class has a unique history of being the first group to experience the exploitation of capitalism:

> When more and more areas were being drawn into world capitalism, development in one area often meant decline of another...As capitalists took the profits accumulated in one place and poured them into new plants and projects in new areas so workers in older industries were thrown out of work and forced to leave their homes...to tramp the roads in search of work. (CDP 1977, 16)

A central theme within the Structuralist discourse is the linking of industrial development to the development of housing, employment and social relations – thus illustrating the irresistible march of history, social forces and class conflict necessitating radical action:

> The costs of industrial change are borne by local working class communities.These communities grew up in response to the demand for labour from new industries, yet over time changes in these industries have destroyed their [working class communities] original role. (CDP 1977, 37)

For proponents of the Structuralist discourse, however, simply defining the 'real' cause of poverty and inequality and refuting competing explanations of poverty linked to pathology and delinquency is not sufficient to effectively educate, agitate and organise the working class. The Structuralist discourse constructs capitalism not only as an oppressive economic system but also as a generator of dominant traditions, norms and values that suppress potential working class dissent: 'there is the unusually clear-cut element in the CDP of social control, the management of unrest' (Cockburn 1977, 125). The East London Claimants Union (ELCU 1974) defines the welfare state as part of the ideological state apparatus and the Structuralist discourse constructs the CDP, the welfare state and the concept of 'participation' in local government decision-making as hegemonic counter-revolutionary devices to co-opt and prevent widespread rebellion (Dearlove 1974, 24–28; Baine 1974, 67; CDP 1977, 37–58; CDP 1978, 37–51). Here is an example of this framing of the CDP and the welfare state:

> By and large those in government are concerned to ensure that collectivities remain their supporters and subjects...The state desires subjects, clients, supporters and helpers, not masters, customers, demanders and disrupters...Numerous groups and individuals accept and absorb this ideology. (Dearlove 1974, 24)

Thus, rather than the CDP and the welfare state being constructed as an important concession won by the organised working class through trade union and social welfare movement struggles, the welfare state is instead constructed by the Structuralist discourse as a weapon of capitalism which engenders false consciousness and undermines revolutionary tendencies among the working classes. To counter these repressive and ideological state apparatuses, the Structuralist discourse argues for the dissolution of state capitalism and the redistribution of wealth and resources via a democratic socialist state:

> [There is a need to recognise] the contradictory nature of state services and...work towards providing a service in the interest of the working class, not capitalism and the state. [This requires] acting collectively to change the structures through which these services are provided so that both workers and consumers have a service which is geared towards their needs and over which they have control. (CDP 1977, 64)

Unsurprisingly perhaps given the focus on the dynamics between state and capital, identity constructions are inadequately articulated in this discourse. The community development professional is constructed as an actor seeking to shed new light on urban poverty in order to educate and inspire the 'working class' to resist the hegemonic practices of the state. Thus the professional appears to be interpellating Gramsci's concept of the organic intellectual:

Partisanship and identification with the concrete problems of the working class and deprived are essential [for the community development professional]. He analyses problems and causes and hopes to join with the people who have these problems to secure improvements. (Baine 1974, 69)

The professional, however, remains ambiguous. Because the Structuralist discourse is an evolution of the Rationalist discourse, it inherits uncertain and contingent constructions of professional. Sitting alongside the professional being an organic intellectual is also the idea that the professional community development worker is infinitely flexible and can be all things to all people:

Community work should not aspire to be a profession in a narrow and traditional sense. By its very nature it has an inter-disciplinary, inter-professional, inter-organisational emphasis. Although a form of practice in its own right, it can and should be developed in a variety of settings and organizations. (Jones and Mayo 1974, xv)

Perhaps part of the problem of this construction of a contingent professional can be found in constructions of local people. Local people in the Structuralist discourse are a silenced, homogenised and passive working class. Here is a typical construction: 'we have to attack directly the sense of powerlessness and the habit of acquiescence with which large numbers of people are oppressed. At present, much of the safety of politicians lies in the passivity of the people' (Lishman 1976, 81). As seen in the British Rationalist discourse and as I demonstrated in Chapter Two in relation to the American Power and Poverty discourses, the consequence of constructing the professional based on notions of 'authenticity', 'expertise' or 'revolution' appears to be the subordination of local people. The Structuralist discourse does not seem to deviate from these discursive patterns. Local people are marginalised in this discourse due to the subject position of 'working class' and the allied assumptions about the political powerlessness of this identity. For example, here is Dearlove (1974, 27) providing another construction of passive and problematic local people:

Of course there is apathy, alienation, defeatism and cynicism, together with a vicious cycle of re-enforcing factors which tend to hold people to their position of poverty, but more in terms of political activity there is a strange acceptance of the position of poverty...What is surprising is not that the poor are politically impotent, it is that some of the poor manage to become politically active for some time.

I think the subject position of 'working class' is a tricky category to sustain because of the ambiguous politics attached to this identity. On the one hand, the working class are impotent and besieged by false consciousness as seen from the quotes above; on the other hand, however, they are the catalyst for social change:

> Workers are residents and consumers [of social welfare services] too...It is around this issue [of urban neighbourhood decline] which communities, and workers suffering the effects of industrial decline, must be organised to press for change, if they are not bear the costs. (Young 1976, 125)

This problematic position of a group constructed as both impotent but also the key constituent for action appears to re-enforce an ambivalent constitution of the community development professional. This contingent subject position of the professional is then made even more uncertain because of the Structuralist discourse's focus on macro-level processes which seem to rob all subjects – both the professional and the working class – of agency.

The construction of problems exclusively through the lens of class and class conflict also serve to misrecognise the experiences of local people. Local people in the Structuralist discourse are homogenised as white, industrial and male (this is in stark contrast to how local people are constituted by the anti-establishment Democracy and Power discourses in America). For example, recall the theme of immigration and how it was constructed as a macro-level problem requiring a state-based solution during this politically salient moment. The experiences of new migrants are misrecognised in the Structuralist discourse as the process of racialisation and discrimination are reconstituted as a problem of capitalism and class conflict:

> [Immigrants] experienced special types of exploitation and humiliation. Encouraged to migrate in the 'boom' fifties, most found themselves stuck with unskilled, dirty or nightshift work...The host community of the older areas, many of them the disappointed elderly who had been left behind, were not easy neighbours to please.

Misunderstandings were fanned into racialism often by national politicians and the media. Immigrants became scapegoats for the very conditions they themselves most suffered from. (CDP 1978, 33)

From the example above we can see how the identity construction of local people as 'working class' is insufficient to capture the multi-dimensional and intersectional experiences of new and settled migrants based on their race, class, gender and legal status (indeed, the above quote can be read as an apologia for white working class racism). Defining all people's experiences through the prism of class misrecognises and homogenises the discrete experiences and perspectives of particular social groups. Furthermore, with these dominant constructions of exploitation only taking place in public spaces, the Structuralist discourse also appears to privilege the male experience in the workplace while marginalising women's experiences in the home and in the community (for a more detailed discussion of this see Chapter Five). A notable exception to this is Cockburn (1977, 176) who concludes her influential account of the local state with an analysis of the politicisation and political organisation of women and how this is an important model for future class struggles: 'A striking feature of the instances of working class action...is the key role that women played in them.'

The constructions of professionals and the working class in the Structuralist discourse are interlinked and self-reinforcing. Contingent constructions of the professional as being an interdisciplinary organic intellectual require a construction of local people as passive and homogenised but with latent agency. That local people are constructed as a passive but potentially active subject make the professional contingent and uncertain. These problematic constructions are made possible by the discursive patterns that privilege the agency of the state and macro-level processes which, as a consequence, undermine the agency of both the professional and local people.

## Conclusions

In this chapter I argued that the dominant discourses of British community development during the politically salient moment of 1968 to 1975 frame social problems and solutions through the lens of the state. Whether through the relatively conservative Rationalist discourse or through the seemingly radical and oppositional Structuralist discourse, potentially destructive macro-level processes are identified to be addressed and it is only the state that is constructed as an effective actor in these complex times. On the surface these two discourses – Rationalist and Structuralist – appear to be in conflict but a closer analysis shows us that these discourses share similar ideas, practices and identity constructions due to their preoccupation with the structure of the state.

Locating both problems and solutions at the institutional level means that the state is the active subject in each of the discourses. As a result of this construction of an activist state, local people – whether named as 'the poor' or the 'working class' – are defined as passive and besieged by social and economic forces beyond their control. Ironically, for two discourses whose concern is seemingly the character of community life and democracy, very little attention is paid to the agency and power of local people to resist and/or change their traditions, their working lives and their social relationships in the face of these new social, technological and economic trends. Indeed, by constructing local people as pathological or experiencing false consciousness it is not clear that either discourse can construct local people in non-hierarchical or anti-oppressive ways. As a result, the state and the professional are privileged in each of the discourses. Even the professional, however, is constituted in an unsatisfactorily way because of the emphasis on macro-level processes. The professional is a contingent and ambivalent subject seeking to reconcile the poor to their problems or unchain them from the bonds of the ideological state apparatus. In either case, constructions of the professional are uncertain and some cases contradictory as the fixation on the state crowds out alternative analyses of identity.

Interestingly in both American and British community development, 1968 does not represent the triumph of radical democracy, equality and justice: it is simply a continuation of the old battles of reformist and progressive politics. Rather than considering new and different spaces and practices of democracy, the micropolitics of community development in each country appears to be fixated on either developing professional expertise to counter the problems of the poor or imposing a homogenising 'revolutionary' ideology that subordinates local people and denies the competing interests and identities of different community groups.

As we turn to a new historical moment it remains uncertain whether community development on either side of the Atlantic can effectively respond to transformative moments in ways that are consistent with its purported goals of democracy and social justice. This failure to respond democratically appears to place community development in a vulnerable position as a new moment unfolds – the rise of the New Right – which actively undermines community development's purported aims and goals. Perhaps community development's inability to promote democracy during a favourable moment in time when its foundational ideas were politically fashionable helps to explain its weak and ineffective responses during a more precarious moment when community development itself falls out of favour.

I will now shift focus by exploring the second politically salient moment in both America and Britain covering the period from 1979 to 1985.

# CHAPTER FOUR

# Community development and the rise of the New Right in America

## Introduction

In the previous two chapters I analysed five community development discourses in America and Britain during the politically salient moment of 1968 to 1975. I demonstrated how, during that moment, the majority of these discourses reproduced unequal and hierarchical relational identities between community development professionals or radical activists and local people. Only one discourse, the Democracy discourse as constituted by the Student Non-violent Coordinating Committee, constructed equalised subject positions between community organisers and local people, however, this particular discourse was successfully marginalised by the other dominant American discourses. My analysis of the micropolitics of that moment suggests that the majority of community development discourses may be unable to effectively construct respectful, democratic and socially just identities within their repertoires. Furthermore, those discourses that attempt to do so appear to be consigned to marginal positions within community development. As I turn to explore a different moment in time, I shall evidence how the discursive patterns I analysed in Chapters Two and Three continue into and are entrenched during the 1980s.

This chapter focuses on the micropolitics of the competing discourses and identities of community development during the rise of the New Right in the United States from 1979 to 1985. I have identified three discourses for analysis. The 'Populist' discourse is constituted by the texts, language and practices of the Alinskyist 'non-ideological' nation-wide neighbourhood movement seeking to curb the perceived power of political, social and economic elites through the decentralisation of decision-making and the building of independent grassroots-based organisations. The 'Partnership' discourse is constituted by the texts, language and practices of technocrats and reformed 1960s radicals seeking to reshape community-based organisations into public–private enterprises whereby 'community development corporations' (CDCs) deliver public services and initiate urban regeneration efforts. Finally, the 'Empowerment' discourse is constituted by the texts, language and practices of second-wave feminist academics and community organisers seeking to construct a new feminist praxis and place gender equality at the heart of community development theory and practice. As I shall demonstrate, these discourses emerge in response to the rise of the New Right and the growing public scepticism about the social and cultural changes of the 1960s and 1970s. As I will argue throughout this chapter, in response to the hegemony of the New Right, the three community development discourses during this moment either adopt the dominant language and practices of the New Right or are marginalised by this political movement.

The chapter begins with a short discussion of the formation and structure of the community development discourses in relation to the rise of the New Right. I shall briefly define and explain the origin of the New Right and then move on to discuss the right-wing backlash against the 1960s reforms in the context of the recession of the late 1970s. I will then turn to analyse the discursive features and identity constructions of the Populist, Partnership and Empowerment discourses and discuss the implications for social justice and equality.

## The New Right in the 1980s

To understand the triumph of the New Right in the 1980s, we need to first look back to the 1964 Lyndon B. Johnson–Barry Goldwater presidential race. Barry Goldwater, a Republican, campaigned as an anti-communist, a free-marketeer and above all, an angry man tired of the tyranny of state over the lives of ordinary people. Here is Goldwater (1964, 1–2) summarising his political philosophy:

> We have lost the brisk pace of diversity and the genius of individual creativity. We are plodding at a pace set by centralised planning, red tape, rules without responsibility, and regimentation without recourse....It is the cause of Republicanism to resist concentrations of power, private or public...It is the cause of Republicanism to ensure that power remains in the hands of the people.
>
> [...]
>
> We Republicans...define government's role where needed at many, many levels, preferably through the one closest to the people involved. Our towns and our cities, then our counties, then our states, then our regional contacts – and

only then, the national government. That, let me remind you, is the ladder of liberty, built by decentralised power.

Goldwater's right-wing populist message about do-gooding elites and technocrats bossing around ordinary people helped to create and legitimate the political environment which would see the New Right capture the presidency in the 1980 election (Diamond 1995, 109–111; Katz 2008, 104–108). For the purposes of my research, I am defining the 'New Right' as a political commitment to populism, libertarianism and traditionalism: 'to be right-wing means to support the state in its capacity as enforcer of order and to oppose the state as a distributor of wealth and power downward and more equitably in society' (Diamond 1995, 9).

Goldwater's failed campaign for the presidency articulated a different role of the state that contrasted sharply with the political projects of both the Kennedy and Johnson Administrations in the 1960s. Rather than the state being defined as 'activist' whereby its role is to intervene in the lives of citizens in order to ensure equality of opportunity, Goldwater's populist message was about shrinking the state and minimising the state's role in everyday life. For him and his right-wing supporters, the state's role was extremely limited to protecting individual liberty and maintaining social order and the existing social hierarchies. Individual liberty for Goldwater draws on Berlin's (1958) notion of 'negative rights' – the right of citizens not to be interfered with in pursuing their interests by other citizens or by the state. The idea of 'positive rights' or the Marshallian idea of social rights is anathema to Goldwater because it seeks to undermine the social order of racial, gender and class hierarchies and it challenges negative rights through a system of taxation and social welfare. For Goldwater, free market capitalism is the symbol and safeguard for negative liberty because it is only in an environment of a decentralised state and a free market that individuals can be radically free to pursue their own interests and succeed or fail based on their individual capabilities.

Goldwater's campaign was a political training ground for young student radicals – in the same way that SNCC and SDS were for left-wing radicals – in which social and fiscal conservatives learned how to organise an emerging grassroots populist base of supporters (Boyte et al. 1986; Fisher 1994; Diamond 1995). The Goldwater campaign invented the practice of 'direct mailing': targeted political advertising to potential supporters. Direct mailing provided partisan information about different local and national hot-button issues, suggested people vote for a specific candidate, encouraged groups to hold hustings and recruited volunteers to campaigns. In this way, the Goldwater campaign and his subsequent defeat tapped into and legitimised growing anxieties among some white people about the rapid social and cultural changes of the 1960s – as seen in the Civil Rights, anti-war, student and feminist movements (Diamond 1995, 113).

Bolstered by a network of think tanks, grassroots organisations and alternative media, by the late 1970s, the New Right was emerging as the dominant political force in the Republican Party and in America more generally. The oil crisis and the sudden end of the post-war economic boom further strengthened rise of the New Right. Here are Boyte et al. (1986, 15) in a particularly helpful characterisation of how the debilitating recession of the mid-1970s fuelled this swing to the right in American public opinion:

> In the context of a growing economic pie [the 30-year post-war economic expansion], Middle American whites could look with sympathy on the struggles and demands of the black underclass...By the end of the decade [the 1970s], the pie had stopped growing and economic worries merged with white opposition to federal initiatives like busing...Liberals, sensitive to plight of the poor and minorities at times gave the impression of insensitivity to the contributions of Lithuanians, Italians, Poles, Irish and others.

Thus two issues coalesced to create an opportunity for the New Right to become dominant in the United States at this time: the economic downturn had given many working-class and middle-class whites a justification to oppose expanding the welfare state (and the higher taxes required to make this expansion possible) and white opposition to government programmes and interventions – like rectifying de facto segregation – could be legitimised based on populist principles of decentralised state power and decision-making. As a result, Ronald Reagan (1981, 1–2) handily defeats Jimmy Carter in the 1980 presidential election through the articulation of a New Right politics that is both libertarian and populist and in doing so he clearly sets out the agenda for his Administration:

> We suffer from the longest and one of the worst sustained inflations in our national history... In this present crisis, government is not the solution to our problem; government is the problem. From time to time we've been tempted to believe that society has become too complex to be managed

by self-rule, that government by an elite group is superior to government for, by, and of the people. Well, if no one among us is capable of governing himself, then who among us has the capacity to govern someone else...The solutions we seek must be equitable, with no one group singled out to pay a higher price.

Reagan's New Right Administration was committed to reducing government expenditure on social welfare and cutting taxes for the rich in a bid to jumpstart the economy to pull America out of the recession. While there are various programmes to which his Administration was committed – namely anti-communism – I am particularly concerned with the Reagan's radical project of social reform in relation to poverty, inequality and community development.

One aspect of the social programme of the New Right was to promote individual liberty and self-reliance by reducing poor people's dependency on what was perceived as a bloated and permissive welfare state (Block et al. 1987; Diamond 1995; O'Connor 1998). Thus, one of the Reagan Administration's primary objectives was the dismantling the welfare state and reducing federal spending on anti-poverty programmes. Here are two quotes that encapsulate the New Right's approach to poor people and the welfare state during this politically salient moment:

> The chloroform of egalitarianism was spread everywhere in the 1970s. Prior American values of self-reliance, personal liberty and competence were heaved overboard...The welfare state had turned many...toiling Americans into parasites and this new class of busybodies [welfare state professionals] lived as super-parasites, deriving nourishment from the dependence of the welfare clients. (Tyrell 1987 quoted in Ehrenreich 1987, 167–8)

> In order to move up, the poor must not only work, they must work harder than the classes above them. Every previous generation of the lower class has made such efforts. But the current poor, white even more than black, are refusing to work hard. (Gilder 1982 quoted in Fisher 1994, 171)

As we can see from the quotes above, the focus in social policy shifts from promoting welfare to workfare: the goal is to reduce dependence on the state and build the self-reliance and independence of the poor through work. Reagan's dismantling of the welfare state resulted in a reduction in the level of cash benefits to poor families and more stringent eligibility requirements in a bid to drastically reduce welfare rolls. Cutting the state also meant that key apparatuses of the previous War on Poverty were abolished. Thus federal funding and support to community development projects and programmes were reduced or withdrawn completely (Block et al. 1987; O'Connor 1998). It is important to note that specific funding streams for particular social welfare activities were deliberately targeted by the new Administration. This was especially the case for community-organising projects working with minority groups in inner-cities and women's health organisations that provided sex education, contraception and abortions (Hyde 1995, 5; Fisher 1994, 171). As a result of these sustained and politically motivated funding cuts, many community development organisations were faced with a Darwinian choice: adapt to the new social order of the New Right or die out.

The micropolitics of the formation and structure of the three discourses I have identified during this moment are shaped in the context of right-wing retrenchment. Depending on how each of the discourses defines the nature of this retrenchment seems to help shape its language, ideas and social practices.

The texts that construct the Populist discourse downplay the New Right as a threat and are thus co-opted by the movement. Texts selected for the Populist discourse include writings from the key architect and proponent of New Populism (Boyte 1980, Boyte 1985, Boyte et al. 1986) discuss the history and development of important New Populist organisations such as the Association of Community Organisations for Reform Now (ACORN), Industrial Areas Foundation (IAF) and Communities Organised for Public Service (COPS) (Delgado 1986; Fisher 1994); and include writings from activist academics charting the reaction of grassroots organisations to the New Right in an influential left-wing journal called *Radical America* (Green and Hunter 1974; Gordon and Hunter 1977; Hunter 1981).

The texts that construct the Partnership discourse attempt to adapt to right-wing retrenchment by adopting the language and practices of the New Right. Texts selected for the Partnership discourse focus on the historical development of and community development practice within community development corporations (Berndt 1977; Peirce and Steinbach 1987; Filner 2001; Stall and Stoecker 1997; Stoecker 1997); the community development corporations' relationship to the New Right (Fisher 1994; O'Connor 1998); and the process of depoliticisation of community development (McKnight and Kretzmann 1984; Delgado 1986; Fisher 1994).

Finally, the texts that construct the Empowerment discourse recognise and seek to oppose right-wing retrenchment. The texts selected for the Empowerment discourse focus on transformations to the study of feminism, gender and 'women' during this moment (Moraga and Anzaldua 1984; West and Zimmerman 1987) and the operation of a feminist praxis in community-based settings (Brandwein 1987; Bookman and Morgen 1988; WOC 1990; Rivera and Erlich 1991; Ferree and Martin 1995).

## The Populist discourse – against ideology

The Populist discourse is constituted by the texts, language and practices of the self-styled movement of 'New Populism' within the field of grassroots activism and community organising. Born out of the collapse of SNCC and the National Welfare Rights Organisation (NWRO), the Populist discourse is an inheritor of the Power discourse and in particular the 'non-ideological' approach to community development as articulated by Alinskyism, which I discussed in Chapter Two. New Populism is defined as:

> a renewed vision of direct democracy coupled with a mistrust of large institutions, both public and private. Such a democratic vision represents a rekindled faith in the citizenry itself, a conviction that, given the means and the information, people can make decisions about the course of their lives; a belief that people can develop a conception of the public interest that does not deny – but rather is nourished by – specific interests. In turn, the building blocks for a revitalised ethos of citizenship are to be found in the voluntary structures of all kinds at the base of American society. (Boyte 1980, 7)

In other words, New Populism is focused on the decentralisation of power from elites to the people in order to revitalise the practice of American democracy. The social practices of New Populism are constructed as:

> cooperative group action by ordinary citizens motivated both by civic idealism and by specific grievances. They [ordinary people] seek some kind of democratisation of

power relations...and they appeal to some implicit popular conviction that there is a broad public good. (Boyte 1980, 8)

Through my analysis of patterns in the language of texts, I understand the Populist discourse to be a reaction against the language and social practices of the Black Power and Poverty discourses I identified and analysed in Chapter Two. The Poverty discourse's expert reformers and the Power discourse's Black Power revolutionaries are defined by the Populist discourse as hostile and anathema to the folkways and traditions of ordinary people because these identity constructions and discursive practices signify distant and unaccountable power and elitist ideological domination. Instead, the Populist discourse constructs itself as a continuation of the American voluntarism tradition and focuses on building alternative and independent community-controlled organisations to represent and affirm the self-interests of citizens. Here is Harry C. Boyte (1980, 9), key architect of New Populism, discussing the problem of elite domination of ordinary people:

> The left can neither understand nor successfully participate in the citizen ferment [of New Populism] if it sees [community] groups instrumentally – as constituencies to be rallied behind a left or 'progressive' agenda...Citizen activism frequently grows directly from traditional and particular group identities that leftists tend to see as 'backwaters' of parochialism – religious and civic traditions, ethnic ties and family relations. In the course of struggle, people often feel deepened appreciation for their heritage, symbols and institutions close to home – a far cry from the abstract cosmopolitanism of the dominant liberal or left imagination...Dialogue that reshapes left categories means recovering activist traditions outside the liberal, socialist, or communist experience.

It seems that the discourse seeks to oppose and marginalise revolutionary politics within the field of community development. In place of these kinds of radical politics, the Populist discourse constructs community traditions and folkways as the authentic basis to build powerful grassroots-based organisations for ordinary people:

> Contemporary citizen organising is more down to earth, more practical, above all more enduring and rooted in the social fabric [of community life]. It seeks to build ongoing

organisations through which people can wield power. It is accompanied by a sense of the rightness, creativity and vitality in people's traditions, folkways and culture that 60s radicals were prone to scorn or dismiss. (Boyte 1980, 139)

The structure of the Populist discourse hinges on three concepts: the idea of 'democracy', a so-called 'non-ideological majoritarian strategy', and a focus on organisational 'victories' rather than the political education of activists. By analysing each of these concepts, I shall demonstrate how the Populist discourse unintentionally reproduces the dominant New Right political practices.

'Democracy' in the Populist discourse is understood as:

popular power – control by the majority of people, with equality of resources sufficient to make such control realisable – and of direct participation by freely cooperating men and women. (Boyte 1980, 175–176)

Democracy is defined as the ability of citizens to self-govern in their own interests. In order to achieve this ideal self-government the greatest threats to citizen self-rule, the state and the market, must be limited. Here are two examples:

The new populism…reflects a continuous effort…to find a successful radical programme that presents, as an alternative to corporate capitalism, a vision for a more cooperative, democratic and decentralised society. (Fisher 1994, 140)

Populist politics has always expressed the belief that government is neither the problem…nor the solution… Government should provide the necessary tools and resource so that particular communities can revitalise themselves and become self-reliant. (Boyte 1985, 2)

At this point I think it is important to highlight how the discourse's construction of democracy perhaps unintentionally echoes the right-wing populist pronouncements of both Goldwater and Reagan. First, from the Boyte quote above, we can see how he imports the language and analysis from one of Reagan's most famous speeches about the problems of 'big government' (which I highlighted at the beginning of this chapter). By constructing the state as a barrier to the realisation of populist democracy – rather than as an arbitrator of equality and justice – the Populist discourse seems to cede a crucial analysis about the state to the New Right. Second, because the Populist discourse defines democracy as a numerical majority and an appreciation and respect of community traditions and folkways, this construction reflects a fundamental New Right tenet of small and decentralised government. (This idea of democracy is very different from the focus on participatory and deliberative democracy as constructed by the Democracy discourse in Chapter Two.) It is unclear why the discourse constructs democracy in this way; however, I think this conceptual framing could be due to a disinclination to recreate the perceived ideological dominations of the 1960s from which the discourse is seeking to distance itself.

On its own, having a populist conception of democracy does not necessarily mean that the Populist discourse is reproducing the political practices of the New Right. This problematic construction of a numerical democracy, however, is closely tied to the second key concept of the Populist discursive repertoire: the 'non-ideological majoritarian strategy'. This strategy focuses on building mass-based, citizen-controlled organisations that are rooted in neighbourhoods, focused on local issues and targeted on winnable issues (Boyte 1980; Boyte et al. 1986; Delgado 1986; Fisher 1993):

> A brand new form of democratic populism is developing in the cities with newly emerging leaders at its head. Aiding these developments is a core of urban organisers [who have learned from the] mistakes of the sixties' movements... Grassroots groups must overcome the divide-and-conquer tactics of the powerful; middle-income people are potential allies, not adversaries; tactics should not alienate the public.
> (Miller 1973 quoted in Boyte 1980, 93)

This strategy is non-ideological because the organisations are built and issues identified and campaigned on based on the 'authentic' interests and concerns of citizens rather than organisers' or outsiders' ideological interpretations of community-based problems and solutions. Here are two interesting examples of the shift away from ideology to populist issues:

> In about 1972, we decided that we should take our resources and experiences and put them at the feet of the community...No line, no Ho Chi Minh, Kim Il Sung, Che. We tried to get back to real, everyday things, to a calm style. We switched issues from Vietnam and Cambodia and just

moved in with the community. (Thompson 1977 quoted in Boyte 1980, 35)

Our philosophy is very closely related to our membership's daily life experience. There's no ideology that instructs what we do. People make decisions and they start moving. (Rathke 1979 quoted in Delgado 1986, 190–1)

The strategy is majoritarian because the organisation is composed of a broad-based constituency which is multi-racial and multi-class and issues are fought for which have broad-based appeal in the neighbourhood:

If we want to develop a majority coalition of Americans who can bust the fat cats who are stealing this country… what we need are independent, mass-based, multi-issue organisations, democratically controlled by their members, taking action on the issues of our time. (Miller 1973 quoted in Boyte 1980, 93)

Through this non-ideological majoritarian strategy, the Populist discourse seeks to further marginalise and silence the Democracy, Black Power and Poverty discourses of the 1960s. The fate of SNCC and NWRO serve as a warning the Populist discursive strategies. SNCC, once the model organisation practising and struggling for participatory democracy, had dramatically collapsed in 1968 through ideological divisions and splits between Leninists, Trotskyites and Black nationalists. NWRO exclusively organised welfare recipients, a disproportionate number of whom were African American women. By 1979 the organisation had floundered because it was unable to expand its base beyond this limited constituency in order to spark a movement for increased federal funding for public services in an era of economic crisis (Piven and Cloward 1979; Delgado 1986; Fisher 1994). Thus, in response to the perceived elitist revolutionary ideology, its destructive effects on grassroots-based organisations and the folly of organising a powerless and easily isolated constituency, the Populist discourse constructs itself as fundamentally different to its forbearers. Here is Wade Rathke (1975 quoted in Fisher 1994, p.148), once the chief organiser of the Association of Community Organisations for Reform Now (ACORN) discussing his positioning of this new organisation that was born out of the demise of NWRO:

> We all knew that we had to break out of the single-issue campaign [of welfare rights]. I wanted to build on a majority constituency rather than on a minority, where the next-door neighbours are in it together, not fighting each other.

Thus in the Populist discourse, the purpose of a community-based organisation, the way issues are framed and the way members are recruited must be understood as a reaction to the social practices of 'failed' community development discourses. I think this is the reason for using a populist understanding of democracy. The non-ideological majoritarian strategy ensures that social problems identified by community development are always framed in terms of the elites – government and corporations – against the (unified and homogenised) people. Potentially divisive issues – especially those related to racial and gender inequalities – are not actively pursued because it would compromise the unity and consensus of the organisation. Only issues with a clearly defined enemy and a clear path to success are defined as viable for mobilising and campaigning. For example:

> We don't cut issues racially where that isn't relevant. There's no point constructing rhetorical enemies who cannot be defeated. Short of race warfare, black people cannot triumph over whites; but whites and blacks can win against real estate agencies…Winning is what is important in organising, it's almost an obsession. (Campbell and Friedman 1978 quoted in Delgado 1986, 194)

It seems that by seeking to build a majority to advocate for a particular community issue requires a broad-based definition of democracy and active avoidance of ideological domination. What is important here to bear in mind is that by supporting the issues and concerns of a numerical majority, this may well lead to an affirmation of the status quo and a marginalisation of issues and groups who challenge established community traditions. Again, this construction of the non-ideological majoritarian concept appears to have a clear resonance with the New Right political philosophy.

The final concept of the Populist discourse is 'victory' which is constructed in two ways. First, building and maintaining a citizen-controlled organisation becomes its own victory for local people – a perpetual self-justification for the process of organising. Here are two examples of this understanding of victory:

> This idea of being organised in a constituency-based organisation...is more important than the particular issue we work on. Again, we might lose or we might win and still the need to be organised remains. (Campbell 1979 quoted in Delgado 1986, 202)

> The very nature of organisational growth and experiences in the process of producing power models its own ideology...For our members, ACORN is a true education in democracy. (Rathke no date, quoted in Boyte 1980, 95)

A permanent organisation, composed of activists ready to react to abuses of power by elites and who can also advance their own self-interest, is constructed as the most effective kind of power people can wield. Targeting winnable issues, with a clear enemy and a clear campaign strategy, builds the confidence of citizens and re-enforces the need for a permanent organisation. People will join and actively participate in an organisation that is perceived to be powerful, formidable and effective.

Focusing on a permanent organisation and on winnable issues creates problems in the discourse, however. From my analysis of texts, there seems to be little sense of how the process of community organising and victory should be linked to a progressive programme for social change. There does not seem to be a distinctive set of social practices within the Populist discourse that would distinguish it from the formidable New Right organising that is also taking place at this time. (Indeed, given this lack of ideology, it is not surprising that the Tea Party of 2008 easily and self-consciously adopts the language and practices of the New Populist movement. For more on this see: Emejulu 2011).

As a result of the structure of this discourse – the focus on a numerical democracy, a non-ideological majoritarian strategy and victory – creates tensions and dislocations within the discourse for which it is unable to resolve. The case of busing, especially in Boston during the late 1970s, illustrates these discursive tensions and the Populist discourse's cooptation by the New Right. Busing, the practice of tackling de facto school segregation by transporting African American children who live in a segregated neighbourhood to predominately white schools in another neighbourhood, was a controversial federal intervention that challenged the will of states and local school boards. Busing was contested by all-white communities for a number of reasons: the practice constituted an important victory for civil rights campaigners seeking an end to inequalities in educational provision; busing was interpreted as an act of unaccountable power by distant government elites which ignored popular sentiments; and, of course, racist whites simply did not want their children to attend integrated schools:

> We have in our midst today a small band of racial agitators, non-native to Boston and a few college radicals who have joined in the conspiracy to tell the people of Boston how to run their schools, their city and their lives. (Day Hicks 1965 quoted in Green and Hunter 1974, 22)

In many ways busing helped spark and sustain the right-wing strain within the New Populist movement by heeding Goldwater's call to re-establish community control and power at the local level. With slogans such as 'Power to the People, fuck the niggers!' single-issue community groups began to organise and mobilise whites against integration (Hunter 1981, 117). The most effective and high profile of these types of populist organisations was Restore Our Alienated Rights (ROAR) which was set up by white business leaders and politicians to stop busing and other federal 'encroachments' in South Boston. ROAR organised and mobilised local whites using the ABCs strategy: anti-abortion, anti-busing and anti-communism (Fisher 1994, 155). ROAR also used strategies and tactics pioneered in the Goldwater campaign, such as direct mail and phone chains, in order to keep local people informed of events and to mobilise them quickly for demonstrations. By using the language and practices of the Populist discourse to support white supremacy, ROAR was effective in building solidarity among the majority Irish Catholic constituency to successfully resist desegregation of South Boston in education, housing and employment (Green and Hunter 1974; Fisher 1994).

The emergence and success of ROAR demonstrates the discursive dislocations of the Populist discourse. A populist, non-ideological, majoritarian approach can be used for either progressive or reactionary practices. By substituting ideology for folkways, by eschewing the political education of activists for the technique of organising and mobilising a constituency, the Populist discourse is easily co-opted by the New Right. Through a wish to avoid the ideological dominations of the past, the discourse appears to cede crucial ground in the practices and politics of community development. In a bid to promote democracy, the discourse unintentionally endorses the tyranny of the majority. Indeed, even after the Populist discourse's language and practices are co-opted by ROAR and other right-wing groups, the discourse attempts to construct clear distinctions between 'right-wing' and 'progressive' populism rather than disavowing reified and essentialised community institutions, community leaders and folkways that can sustain injustice and inequality:

> On the individual level neither right-wing nor progressive populism often exists in a pure form. People may have one view on economic issues, another view on social issues and another view on foreign policy...but with all these complexities there are broad values and responses emerging that make two kinds of populism increasingly identifiable. (Boyte et al. 1986, 10)

I now want to explore the identity constructions constituted by this discourse. A community organiser identity is constructed who facilitates the will of the people and helps people make sense of the world and their experiences within it. For example, here is Delgado (1986, 82) discussing the role of the organiser in this way:

> An organiser is fighting a battle to win not simply campaigns but people's minds...Organisers must use the process of organising to expand the collective experiences of community residents and use [the] organisation to validate redefined collective perceptions of how the world works... Community organisers are social reconstructionists. Their role is to develop the ability of people to understand the world so that they can act in it.

In contrast to the Democracy discourse, the Populist organiser is not necessarily committed to consensus-based decision-making. That would compromise the building of a majority around winnable issues. Instead the Populist organiser is committed to building an organisation that reflects the priorities of a broad-based constituency.

The community organiser is also constructed as a technician concerned with mechanics of building and maintaining a community-based organisation. For example: 'the organiser [is] an "expert" who practices a method, almost a "science", of organising' (Fisher 1994, 153). The community organiser has been stripped of meaning and is a non-ideological worker perfecting the craft of organisation-building. What that organisation is for, where it is positioned politically and how it frames social problems is downplayed within the discourse. With the community organiser concerned with technique and victories rather than broader ideological and political issues, the organiser, ironically, fails to build and mobilise the democratic majority to which it aspires.

For example, Adamson (1980 quoted in Delgado 1986, 195–6), a vocal critic of non-ideological Populist politics, argues:

> For young Blacks, if you want to get into what's happening in your community, an ACORN or a Fair Share is not the place to do it...The organisations are inadvertently racist... What they do is they treat everybody the same way. If you don't take into account the fact that there are real differences culturally, you're going to have problems...The hierarchy [of these organisations] is reflective of essentially what society is; it's all white and mostly male.

Two opposing identities are also constructed in this discourse: elites wielding unaccountable power and the reified 'people'. As previously discussed, New Populism is a reactionary movement against three types of elites: government, corporate and revolutionary. Interestingly, not a lot of distinction is made between these three very different types of elites because the discourse constructs them as having the same harmful impact: undermining the self-determination of the people:

> While it [New Populism] is critical of elements of the economic system, it sees bigness and unaccountable power, rather than capitalism, as the fundamental problem...Its fundamental analysis is that unchecked power has become concentrated in the hands of a very small number of people who are at the helm of the major corporations of the nation. Because government remains unaccountable to most people, it too, along with business is part of the problem. (Fisher 1994, 139)

Whether it is domination through privatisation, through the centralisation of state power or through language and ideas, all elites prevent the people from making decisions on issues that are important to them.

This construction of elites is tactically ambiguous in the discourse in order to facilitate solidarity and organisation building by organisers at the neighbourhood level. The othering of elites is problematic, however, not just because it has a knock on effect of homogenising 'the people' but because this construction feeds easily into the reactionary politics of the New Right and makes it very difficult to critique oppressive and dominating community institutions and norms using the language and social practices of the Populist discourse.

The third identity construction in the discourse is a reified and homogenised 'people'. The people are all the same: they are civic-minded, they share the same interests and they are not in conflict with each other over power and resources. The people are reified through the way in which traditions, folkways and community-based institutions are fetishised in the discourse. Here are two examples:

> Populism…grows from the living fabric of communities seeking to control the forces that threaten to overwhelm them. Populism…is ultimately about values and cultural meanings. Rather than drawing its base from large organisations…in which people are cut off from their family roots and communal ties, populist politics finds its power and vision in the institutions integral to social life: churches, synagogues, neighbourhood organisations, union locals. (Boyte 1985, 1)

> ACORN has a line: rather than organising around racism, we involved our members in campaigns that affect all low and moderate income people, building solidarity…Our people have common problems and they try to help one another, not kick them in the butt because they're black or Catholic or something. (Delgado 1986, 193)

Like the construction of elites, this construction of 'the people' appears to be tactical: by defining everyone as the same and by emphasising the essential goodness of community structures, these constructions aim to make it easier to build solidarity and organise competing groups for collective action. The problem, however, is that the very real conflicts, contradictions and interests between different groups are ignored for the sake of organisation building. As we have seen, controversial issues are avoided or reframed to make them palpable to the majority interests and as a result, crucial minority and single issues are silenced. As I will discuss later, the Empowerment discourse can be seen as a reaction to the silence of race, class and gender issues in the Populist discourse. Ironically, by choosing a phantom and mythical majority, the Populist discourse renders itself a weak, fractured and minority-interest discourse that is vulnerable to cooptation by the New Right.

I will now move on to analyse the structure and identity constructions of the Partnership discourse.

## The decline of radicalism in the Partnership discourse

In contrast to the Populist discourse, the Partnership discourse should be interpreted as a radical departure in the ideas, language and practices of community development. Although contradictory, the Populist discourse has embedded in its practices flawed but recognisable orientations to democracy, equality and social justice. My analysis of patterns in the language of the Partnership discourse, however, reveals a new and problematic direction for community development in the United States.

The Partnership discourse is constituted by the ideas, language and practices of the funders, partners and practitioners of the second and third generation of community development corporations (CDCs). Pioneered in Brooklyn, championed by then Attorney General Robert Kennedy and funded by Johnson's War on Poverty programmes in 1966, CDCs were conceived as innovative approaches to neighbourhood decline and the culture of poverty in inner cities. CDCs would:

> join the resources, expertise and energy of American private enterprise with those of the public sector in a special attack on the problems of the nation's urban areas having the largest concentration of poverty. (Economic Opportunity Amendment 1966 quoted in Filner 2001, 2)

Growing from a dozen first generation demonstration projects in the late 1960s to several hundred second generation projects in the 1970s to between 3,000 to 5,000 third generation projects in the 1980s, CDCs were seen as an innovative solution to two important challenges facing community development: the Reagan Administration's funding cuts to social welfare programmes and the rapid decline and deterioration of inner-city infrastructure (Berndt 1977, 110–115; Peirce and Steinbach 1987, 19–29).

Indeed the federal funding cuts could not have come at a worse time for the inner-cities of America in the early 1980s. Already weakened by the recession and the out-migration of jobs and the middle class tax base to the suburbs, cities, especially those in the rustbelt, were unable to cope with reduced federal spending. As a result, several cities adopted a policy of 'planned shrinkage': a reduction in social welfare spending in declining inner city areas to encourage the out-migration of poor residents and to entice businesses and the gentrifying middle classes back to urban areas through tax breaks and economic development projects (Block et al. 1987, 135; Fisher 1994, 136–7). As a result of these developments, community-based organisations sought to restructure themselves in order to get access to new funding sources for regeneration work.

As the number of CDCs proliferate in the search for new funding sources, 'community development' as I have defined and understood it in terms of this book, undergoes a dramatic transformation. By seeking to build viable partnerships between poor communities, the private sector and the state, the Partnership discourse radically reconstructs the language and practices of community development. This transformation is apparent in two key patterns in the language of the Partnership discourse: a new emphasis on pragmatism and the depoliticisation of the practices of community development. CDCs expand out of organisational survival tactics and the discourse articulates a new vision for community development by focusing on the pragmatism of the decision to change what community development means and the way in which it is perceived by institutional actors and the general public. For example, here are Peirce and Steinbach (1987, 9), key proponents of CDCs, reconstructing the meaning and purpose of community development:

> This [CDC] movement...is quintessentially American. It mirrors the qualities of our society that so impressed Alexis de Tocqueville in the 1830s: our penchant for innovative civic associations, our belief that individuals can bring about change, our openness to risk taking and to bridging line of class, ideology and party. CDCs...have become a major component of corrective capitalism; in this free-enterprise nation they are finding ways to open doors to classes and individuals otherwise excluded from the American dream.

The Partnership discourse constructs pragmatism as the adoption of the ideas and social practices of the New Right particularly in relation to neoliberalism:

> Many of today's CDCs are becoming adept at hooking into the 1980s culture of small businesses, entrepreneurial growth and building capacity for indigenous economic development in communities long plagued by poverty and dependency. (Peirce and Steinbach 1987, 30–1)

Part of the innovation of the Partnership discourse is its restructuring of the language and practices of community development from *social justice for poor people* to *entrepreneurship for poor neighbourhoods*:

> Community members who become managers, directors of boards [of CDCs] and presidents of businesses learn new skills and become participants rather than observers of the system. Through participation they…learn about the system and therefore become better able to cope with its complexities…[and as a result] residents shed their feelings of inadequacy and helplessness. (Berndt 1977, 34)

By supporting the expansion of capitalism in poor neighbourhoods and by linguistically transforming poor people into latent capitalists, the Partnership discourse seeks to reconstruct traditional notions of empowerment – thus providing further legitimacy for its dramatic discursive shifts. Rather than empowerment being defined as the redistribution of power, agency and decision-making, the Partnership discourse defines empowerment on neoliberal terms, as the development of an entrepreneurial spirit in order to enjoy and exploit the opportunity of free-market capitalism. For example:

> The conception [of CDCs] was that being poor is not an individual affair but rather a systemic disease that afflicts whole communities. Deteriorated housing, impaired health, nonexistent or low wages, the welfare assault on self-respect…all these feed on each other…[Thus the need for] a community based and comprehensive approach to improving the local economy rather than trying desperately somehow to rebuild each individual. (Perry no date, quoted in Peirce and Steinbach 1987, 21–2)

Empowerment is constructed in this discourse as submitting to neoliberalism rather than seeking to oppose it. By understanding and working for the expansion of capitalism, local people will never again be at the mercy of economic forces that seek to impoverish them.

Furthermore, what makes the Partnership discourse new and different is its disavowal of its radical forbearers and the subsequent depoliticisation of its language and practices. For example, Peirce and Steinbach (1987, 8), two writers hired by the Ford Foundation to promote CDCs in order to attract more funding from the federal government and the private sector argue:

For many Americans, the mention of 'community organisation' conjures up 1960s images of radicals storming city hall, of civil rights marches, anti-Vietnam protest, lettuce boycotts and distrust of anyone in a business suit. In fact, many of today's successful CDCs had their roots in that period. But with rare exceptions, the 1960s are now as much history for them as for the rest of American society.

With the acceptance of the new social and economic order of the New Right, the Partnership discourse abandons practices of controversy, dissent and opposition – anything that might compromise the delicate balance of new collaborators and new funders from the private sector:

In the 1970s we were activists, mostly out of the civil rights movement... We may be tending now, with more Harvard and Wharton [business school] grads, to be approaching development with less 'political' sense. It may be creating a complacency among us... It's harder to fight with Sun Oil or a Bell Tel when you want to look and act like them. (Rubin 1987 quoted in Peirce and Steinbach 1987, 34)

Here is another example of the depoliticisation of community development social practices in the discourse:

CDCs have reassessed the marketplace... Now we are understanding what will fly in this climate – and what won't.

[...]

Today you have to find ways to resemble the real for-profit world... otherwise you won't be around.

[...]

We no longer take a 'gimme, gimme' attitude. Now we are learning how to infiltrate into the system. We've learned to be much more creative. (Peirce and Steinbach 1987, 29–30)

I will now demonstrate how identity constructions in the Partnership discourse re-enforce this shift away from recognisable forms of community development towards the adoption of New Right language and practices.

There is a two-pronged identity construction in the Partnership discourse: the reformed radical and the technical expert. The reformed radical is constructed as a pragmatic, depoliticised and non-threatening activist primarily driven by concern about neighbourhood decline. This concern translates into a need to shift away from 'old-fashioned' approaches to community development as seen in the Democracy, Power and Populist discourses and focusing on non-confrontational activities that build resilience and productive capacities of poor people for self-help. For example: '[Activists should not be] out in the streets making symbolic statements, when you can be in the boardroom negotiating specific agreements that win for your neighbourhoods' (Trapp 1992 quoted in Fisher 1994, 191).

This chastened activist is also a technical expert who will help poor people build self-reliance. With the technical skill to assemble a wide range of partners to fund complex regeneration projects, the activist reformer is invested with agency to solve the problems of the poor. For example:

> The directors of today's community development organisations are savvy and well-schooled in deal making. Many have worked in the private sector or in government. Some have advanced business or law degrees. Quite a few grew up in the neighbourhoods they are now trying to revive. They manifest a special quality...Many would succeed, one mayor told us, at running even the largest private corporations...They are practitioners with sophistication and technical capacity. They are people programmed for success, trying to instil that notion in communities where failure is the norm. (Peirce and Steinbach 1987, 8)

As we have seen with previous discourses, the Partnership discourse invests the community development professional with agency. The professional is constructed as a subject with the capabilities to tackle the problems in poor neighbourhoods. As a consequence, this discourse constitutes one key opposing identity: the invisible and passive poor. On the one hand, people living in poverty are rendered invisible by this discourse. Local people are removed from discussions about redevelopment and regeneration and replaced with an abstract notion of a neighbourhood that is empty of people. By disappearing the poor, the discourse is able to construct itself as pragmatic and non-threatening to its sceptical but much needed government and private sector funders. I am surprised that there are so few references to 'the poor' in this discourse. The focus in this discourse is about the reconstruction of the idea of community development from activism to capitalist development. From the references to the poor that do exist (there are some scattered throughout the quotes in this section of the chapter), it is clear that the poor are constructed as a passive and objectified mass. The only way that the poor can develop agency is by being acted on by the professional and learning the technical capitalist know-how to overcome dependency and failure. For example: 'CDCs strive to rebuild dilapidated housing, to kindle a spark of economic vitality, to reverse residents' overwhelming sense of negativism and isolation' (Peirce and Steinbach 1987, 13).

The Partnership discourse seeks to transform foundational ideas, practices and identities of community development. By seeking to reconcile itself to the dominant discourse of the New Right, the discourse, supports, re-enforces and expands the hegemony of this political philosophy.

I will now turn to analyse the final discourse during this politically salient moment in time.

## The Empowerment discourse: a transformational approach?

The Empowerment discourse is constituted by the texts, language and practices of second-wave feminist theorists and community organisers seeking to reclaim, revalue and reassert the hidden history and contemporary practices of working class and minority ethnic women activists in grassroots politics and community development. This discourse is oppositional to the New Right, Populist and Partnership discourses because the Empowerment discourse seeks to transform the nature of politics and by doing so, attempt to undermine those dominant discursive practices that misrecognise and subordinate working class and minority ethnic women, their interests and their agency:

> Working class women defy the portrayal of women so common in the popular press as passive, politically disinterested, unskilled or ineffectual...For these women, empowerment begins when they change their ideas about the causes of their powerlessness, when they recognise the systemic forces that oppress them and when they act to

change the conditions of their lives. (Bookman and Morgen 1988, 3–4)

By reclaiming the voices and experiences of women in community development, the Empowerment discourse seeks to construct a feminist praxis whereby a diverse range of working class and minority ethnic women can articulate, analyse and take action on the issues that are important to them and as a result, dismantle the personal, social, and economic structures that foster their oppression:

> The overarching goal of feminist [community] organising is the elimination of permanent power hierarchies between all people which can prevent them from realising their human potential. The objective of feminist approaches is to reduce sexism, racism and other forms of oppression through the process of empowerment which seeks individual liberation through collective activity embracing both personal and social change. (Gutierrez and Lewis 1992, p.116)

The Empowerment discourse is a product of, is reproduced by and in turn, helps produce the language and practices of the second-wave feminist movement in the United States. While it is beyond the bounds of this book to provide a detailed analysis the origin and politics of the second-wave movement, it is important to highlight the controversies and tensions within wider feminist politics in order to understand the language, structure and practices of the Empowerment discourse.

The second-wave movement was incubated and fostered by women's experiences in civil rights and New Left organisations of the 1960s. Working in SNCC, SDS and other Civil Rights, anti-war and student organisations, women (and men) were learning the processes and tactics of organisation-building, community engagement, direct action and leadership development. Women were also learning, however, how their distinct interests *as women* were ignored, devalued or dismissed and how they *as women* were subordinated in male dominated revolutionary organisations, networks and movements. The second-wave feminist movement was born out of women's frustrations of having to put their particular interests behind class-based or race-based interests deemed more important or more foundational to achieving social justice (for a detailed discussion of the history of the American movement see Evans 1980 and Echols 1989).

Part of the process of maturation for the second-wave movement in the 1970s was the on-going struggle to define the nature of the movement: what the category of 'woman' means, whose voices were heard and whose interests and issues the movement reflects. The emergence of different forms of feminisms – Black, lesbian, Chicana – for example, reflects these internal debates. An on-going tension within the movement – which also permeates the Empowerment discourse – concerns the problem of reification of women and their interests. Women of colour critiqued the tendency of some white feminists to ignore, devalue or homogenise women's interests linked to race, caste, ethnicity and class and only legitimise, reflect and take action on white middle-class women's issues. For example:

> Black, other Third World and working women have been involved in the feminist movement from the start, but… racism and elitism within the movement itself have served to obscure our participation…It was our experience and disillusionment with these liberation movements…that led to the need to develop a politics that was anti-racist, unlike those of white women and anti-sexist, unlike those of black and white men, (Combahee River Collective 1977, 2)

The Empowerment discourse represents an attempt by some feminist theorists and community activists to reconcile these political conflicts within the second-wave feminist movement and construct new identities and practices for feminism. In order to build a new feminist praxis, the Empowerment discourse seeks to first reconstruct the ideas of politics, power, and ideology and then apply these concepts to the nature of community development.

A key practice of the Empowerment discourse is the redefinition of 'politics' and the nature of political spaces. Building on the concept that the 'personal is political', the discourse reconstructs the binary of public/private spaces. Rather than public spaces being the only legitimate realm for debate and action, private, domestic and community spaces – the spaces that most women occupy and organise their lives around – are also defined as spaces for the practice of politics. Ackelsberg (1988, 299–301), writing about the legitimacy of politicised community spaces, argues:

> What is defined as 'political' – that is, as publicly relevant – determines what is available for open discussion, the categories in which people come to understand their experience and the possibilities they see as resistance…The full effect of these ideological separations [between public

and private spaces] limits both the agenda of politics and the range of likely participants…Many women, as a result, have found that the issues of greatest concern to them (safe neighbourhoods, decent jobs, day care and education for their children, availability of health care) have been treated as irrelevant or of secondary significance to politics.

By reconceptualising the spaces where politics is practiced and by politicising private issues not normally defined as part of legitimate political inquiry and debate, the discourse is then able reclaim and redefine women's work in the private sphere as political and worthy of analysis and struggle:

> The basis for women's collective action…was to be found in the daily round of domestic responsibilities…It was in these small groups that patterns of cooperation, communication and analysis were established and that the value of collective effort…was experienced…An emphasis on one's responsibilities to kin was extended to responsibilities for the community. (Susser 1988, 262)

Importantly, the Empowerment discourse also seeks to redefine politics by constructing an intersectional approach to the categories of race, class and gender in its new conception of politics. By recognising how different social categories are reproductive systems of oppression that cannot be separated, the discourse critiques other feminist discourses that do not attempt these intersectional analyses:

> Efforts are made to bridge differences between women based on such factors as race, class, physical ability and sexuality orientation with the guiding principle that diversity is strength…Feminist practitioners will not only strive to eliminate racism, classism, heterosexism, anti-semitism, ableism and other systems of oppression and exploitation, but will affirm the need for diversity by actively reaching out to achieve it. (Gutierrez and Lewis 1992, 117)

Through the redefinition of politics, political activity and viable political issues, the discourse then reconstructs the nature and practice of power. Dominant understandings of power are constructed as counter-productive and unable to capture how working class and minority ethnic women experience and use their power. Power, as defined in the Power and Populist discourses, for example, is often defined as a zero-sum. The amount of power that exists is finite and the only way for powerless people to gain power is to take it away from the powerful. This way of constructing power is to assume destructive conflict and confrontation between the 'powerless' and 'powerful'. The Empowerment discourse seeks to redefine the nature of power in order to better understand how women use power:

> Feminism embraces a win–win approach to power…Power is infinite…In such a case I do not lose power if you are also empowered. To convert a situation into a 'win–win' game one must not avoid conflict but rather one must use the creative resolution of conflict. (Brandwein 1987, 117)

Because a key practice of the Empowerment discourse is the reconstruction of spaces and practices of politics, it defines power as a generative and relational process based on the 'web of relationships' working class and minority ethnic women build for themselves for resilience, survival and solidarity in the private and community sphere. Thus, the way working class and minority ethnic women obtain and use power is through the practice of empowerment:

> In women-centered organising, power begins in the private sphere of relationships, and thus is not conceptualised as zero–sum, but as limitless and collective…Empowerment is a developmental process that includes building skills through repetitive cycles of action and reflection which evoke new skills and understandings, which in turn provoke new and more effective actions. (Stall and Stoecker 1997, 12)

By grounding power in the private spaces women occupy and by redefining power as the ability to collectively analyse and take action on important issues, the Empowerment discourse seeks to construct a new feminist community development praxis in opposition to both the New Right and other competing community development discourses during this politically salient moment. Rather than seeking to reconcile itself to the hegemony of the New Right, the Empowerment discourse attempts to mobilise its new conception of politics in order for working class and minority ethnic women to resist the New Right and counter domination by other competing discourses. By linking public and private spaces and demonstrating how practices in one space impact on the other; by supporting the networks and relationships that women build for themselves and from which they derive solidarity; and by fostering personal and collective empowerment, the discourse seeks to put forward a new way of working with women and a new way to struggle for social justice:

> Women's coming to political consciousness...may be more a phenomenon of relationship and connection...It is in and through networks...that most women engage in collaborative activity and through that activity, can begin to experience themselves as confident, competent beings; citizens in a democratic polity...Political life is community life; politics is attending to the quality of life in households, communities and workplaces (Ackelsberg 1988, 306–8)

Thus the Empowerment discourse articulates a new feminist praxis which builds and sustains women's organic networks. These networks in turn support a process of collective analysis and action on issues that are important to women. As a result of this process, a sense of personal and collective empowerment may result. Unlike in the Populist discourse, victory is not of central importance in this discourse. Instead, the Empowerment discourse interpellates the practices of the Democracy discourse whereby the process of collective education and building agency is of equal importance as the outcome.

The oppositional nature of the Empowerment discourse can be seen in its identity constructions. Like the Democracy discourse that I discussed in Chapter Two, the Empowerment discourse is seeking to break down the hierarchical relations between the community organiser and the groups with whom she works. The feminist organiser identifies with and may well be a member of the community or group of women that she seeks to organise:

> Since community workers are primarily political actors who view their client constituencies as peers, they do not see professional expertise and occupational status as legitimate bases for socio-political differentiation. Instead, professional expertise and training are aspects of their commitment to the community. (Gilkes 1988, 56)

Because of this breakdown of traditional binary identity constructions, the Empowerment discourse constructs working-class and minority ethnic women with agency and with equal status to the community organiser. Because the discourse does not make a distinction between the 'organiser' and 'community' subject positions, this allows for the construction of identities based on equality, justice and respect. Importantly, the Empowerment discourse interpellates the marginalised Democracy discourse by using its language of community organisers as facilitators and women as indigenous leaders:

> Effective feminist organising with women of colour requires that women of colour be in leadership roles...The organiser must be willing to serve as a facilitator... Feminist organisers should work with these indigenous leaders and learn from them the most effective ways of working with particular communities. (Gutierrez and Lewis 1992, 124–8)

These identity constructions are in direct contrast to the Populist and Partnership discourses that continue the tradition constructing a dominating professional and subordinate local people.

The Empowerment discourse's identity constructions are not without problems, however. An on-going discursive tension within the wider feminist discourse and within the Empowerment discourse in particular can be seen in the reification and essentialising of the subject position of 'women'. For example, the Women Organisers' Collective (WOC 1990, 13–15) discusses the need for SNCC-style non-hierarchical organisational and leadership structures which are supportive of women's ways of working in community organisations:

> Women are particularly suited for this more egalitarian form of leadership because women have a more collegial style and are more 'sisterly'... We are generally more flexible and open to new ideas. We can admit our imperfections, which takes the pressure off, and we can tolerate criticism...We don't aspire to obtain leadership positions and then to stay in them until we are thrown out or until we die.

By undertaking this process of reification, the Empowerment discourse seems to develop a new form of binary identity constructions based on women/men instead of the traditional community development binary of practitioner/local people. Interestingly, the Empowerment discourse does attempt to address the issue of reification by looking to the innovative ways in which women work together – rather than relying on suspect pronouncements about the biological differences between women and men:

> That feminist strategy [of reification] – which tends to define these [women's] values as rooted in biologically based sex difference...runs the risk of biologistic reductionism, of reinstituting traditional male–female dichotomies in a new guise. A focus on communities and networks offers us another language, one not necessarily burdened with gender-based connotations. (Ackelsberg 1988, 309)

One key opposing identity is constructed in this discourse: the technical professional. The Empowerment discourse appears to conflate the confrontational Alinskyist organiser with the bureaucratic professional. These two identities are combined, it seems to me, because they both have a similar impact of subordinating working class and minority ethnic women and their interests. For example:

> Feminist principles are not encouraged or employed by organisers and feminist practices are used only in isolated settings...There are conflicts between the collective, connected style being emphasised in consciousness-raising groups and the traditional, aggressive Alinsky-style of organising that is taught in most [sic] curriculums. (WOC 1990, 1)

Through a focus on technique – whether that be the Populist discourse's focus on organisation building or the Partnership discourse's focus on regeneration or remote institutional actors unable to recognise the distinct interests of working class and minority ethnic women – these experts are constructed as threats to the self-determination of women.

Despite the Empowerment discourse's attempt to construct a new model for community development; to adopt an intersectional approach to race, class and gender; and to reconceptualise the nature of power and empowerment, it is not clear how effective it is in opposing the New Right and the other community development discourses during this moment in time. Certainly, the Empowerment discourse is successful in creating space for thinking and practising community development by reclaiming the discursive practices of the marginalised Democracy discourse. Given the subsequent triumph of the New Right in dismantling the welfare state and the growing hegemony of the Partnership discourse as a legitimate and viable 'alternative' to traditional approaches to community development, however, it is doubtful how successful the Empowerment discourse is in translating its approach in the private sphere into the public sphere that the other discourses occupy.

## Conclusions

As the dominant political movement of the late 1970s and the 1980s, the New Right fundamentally transforms the discourses of American community development. A combination of the recession and a backlash against an activist welfare state helps to feed and sustain the right-wing shift in American public opinion and bolster the hegemony of the New Right. The three community development discourses during this moment in time, for different reasons, are each ineffective in opposing the New Right.

The Populist discourse retreats by collapsing into itself. By seeking to organise and mobilise a 'majority' the discourse reifies its targeted constituents thus limiting its appeal and ironically ensuring that only a minority of activists would be mobilised to oppose the New Right. As a result, the 'non-ideological' Populist discourse is co-opted by the New Right. The Partnership discourse, on the other hand, capitulates when confronted with the hegemonic practices of the New Right. In order to avoid marginalisation, this discourse adopts the ideas and practices of the New Right through its focus on capitalist development of poor neighbourhoods. By pragmatically accepting the dominance of the New Right, the Partnership discourse ensures its future survival – but at a very heavy cost for community development and communities living in poverty. The Empowerment discourse creates a new community development praxis whereby feminist theory, the recognition of difference and a reconstruction of power and politics are emphasised rather than eschewed. It appears that this discourse has been ineffective in countering a New Right movement operating and sustained by traditional politics in public spaces, however.

Through my analysis of this moment and these discourses, I have identified clear trends in the micropolitics of community development. As I demonstrated in Chapters Two and Three, the majority of community development discourses create disempowering and undemocratic identity constructions and social practices with regards to practitioners and local people. Practitioners are constructed as active agents while local people are constructed as homogenised and passive objects to be acted on by professionals. Whether community development disavows revolutionary politics or adopts right-wing politics, it cannot seem to escape from a fundamental problem of constructing the professional as an active subject and local people as a passive object. Although the Empowerment discourse occupies a marginal position in community development during this moment, like the Democracy discourse in Chapter Two, it provides an alternative conception about the nature of community development and its relationship to equality and social justice. By constructing local people as active and competent agents and recognising differences among local people, the Empowerment discourse provides an important oppositional stance to the problematic constructions of the Populist and Partnership discourses.

I will now turn to analyse the community development discourses during the politically salient moment of 1979 to 1985 in Britain in order to compare the structure and operation of these discourses in the context of Thatcherism and the crisis in left-wing politics in that country.

# CHAPTER FIVE

# From radicalism to realism: rethinking community development in a post-Marxist Britain

## Introduction

In the last chapter, I demonstrated how the New Right exerted a powerful influence over the micropolitics of American community development during the 1970s and 1980s. I analysed how one discourse downplayed the threat of the New Right and was ultimately co-opted by this movement. Another discourse sought accommodation with the New Right by adopting its language and social practices and subsequently abandoned key concepts traditionally linked to community development. Only one discourse, linked to anti-racist feminism, attempted to oppose the hegemony of the New Right through a focus on women's empowerment. In this chapter I will examine how British community development discourses fare during the 1979 to 1985 politically salient moment. I have identified two discourses for analysis. The 'post-Marxist' discourse is constituted by the texts, language and practices of community development theorists and practitioners seeking to restructure the dominant Marxist praxis of 'radical' community development in order to shift away from the perceived economic determinism and dogmatism of classical Marxism and construct a new praxis based on more complex analyses of the welfare state and of 'working class' experiences. In contrast this, the 'Realist' discourse is constituted by the texts, language and practices of community development theorists and practitioners who seek to subvert and marginalise the dominant Marxist discourse and instead construct a new community development praxis based on professionalism in social administration and neighbourhood-based work.

In this chapter I shall argue that these two discourses emerge in response to two important developments: a major crisis in left-wing politics and the rise of the New Right as embodied in Margaret Thatcher's Government. In contrast to American community development during this moment in time, the micropolitics of British community development are oriented towards reconciling the internal struggles plaguing left-wing politics. Rather than left-wing politics being abandoned by some discourses as I demonstrated in Chapter Four in the US context, I will argue that community development in the UK must contend with the processes of Marxism being altered by new social movements such as second-wave feminism and, to a lesser extent, new political philosophies such as post-structuralism and postmodernism. In addition, I will discuss how community development is forced to respond to the deteriorating state of urban neighbourhoods and rising unemployment levels which Marxist community development had been unable to influence or affect. I will also argue that while the New Right does heavily influence this moment, Thatcher's attack on the welfare state should be understood as an example that both community development discourses use to illustrate the failure of Marxist analyses of the 'state' and the 'working class' to predict, explain or counter these events.[7]

## The crisis of the left and the problem of 'actual existing socialism'

While it is beyond the scope of this book to provide a detailed history of the crisis of socialist politics in Britain, I will focus on some of the key disputes that help to shape the micropolitics of community development during this moment. The political crisis can be attributed to four interconnected developments: the backlash against classical Marxist theory and practice; the emergence of new social movements – particularly feminism; the rise of the 'post-industrial' society and the growing popular support for the New Right.

Perhaps the most important influence on the micropolitics of British community development at this time is that in broader socialist politics, classical Marxism was moving out of favour. Theorists, activists and trade unionists were beginning to have doubts about the orthodoxy of theory and practice that Marxism seemed to demand (Gorz 1980; Laclau and Mouffe 2001; Hall 1988; Sim 2001). These sceptics of classical Marxism wished to preserve the critique of capitalism and capitalist societies that Marxism provides, but move beyond the dogmatism of traditional Marxist politics and practices. The nature of the debates about Marxism isrooted in both theory and practice. In terms of theory, the 'grand narrative' of Marxism seemed to require that everyday life be understood only in terms of class conflict between the proletariat and

---

[7]     I will discuss the influence of Thatcherism on British community development in far greater detail in Chapter Seven.

the bourgeoisie. Consequently, sceptics argued, Marxism's central focus on class silences certain experiences and perspectives – particularly those of women and minority ethnic groups. In practice, Marxist dogma was experienced in the bureaucratic hierarchies of 'revolutionary' socialist parties and in the repressive countries of the Soviet bloc:

> The image of Marxism that prevails [during this time] is of a system that is authoritarian, totalitarian, control-obsessed and hypocritical. [Sceptics] have given up trying to bridge the gap between theory and reality that in their eyes makes a mockery of Marxism's liberationist political pretensions. (Sim 2001, 3)

In light of the 'actual existing socialism' of Stalinism, sceptics of classical Marxism were seeking a new path. As Stuart Hall (1988, 184–5) argues:

> The actuality of Stalinism and its aftermath has added the tragic dimension to the language of socialism: the stark possibility of failure. The socialist experiment can go wildly and disastrously wrong…In our struggle to realise a proper kind of socialism, we have to first explain – and not explain away – the other kind: the kind where, in the name of the workers' state, the working class is actually shot down in the streets, as is happening at this very moment to Polish Solidarity in Gdansk.

This questioning of the democratic principles of Marxism is directly connected to the second key factor of the political crisis: the emergence of new social movements. Because classical Marxism suppresses pluralist ideas of difference, it tends to homogenise the nature of lived experiences of people by ascribing them the subject position of 'working class'. This totalising subject position privileges class above all other identities and also assumes a level of unity, consensus and agreement among ordinary people. Socialist sceptics found the idea of the 'working class' to be a distorting myth that should be abandoned for more realistic and heterogeneous understandings of ordinary people. Here is an influential discussion of the problems of the term 'working class' by Ernesto Laclau and Chantal Mouffe (1985, 2):

> What is now in crisis is a whole conception of socialism which rests upon the ontological centrality of the working class…The illusory prospect of a perfectly unitary and

homogeneous collective will that will render pointless the moment of politics. The plural and multifarious character of contemporary social struggles has finally dissolved the last foundation for that political imaginary.

Given both the influence and currency of feminist and anti-racist ideas during this moment in time, sceptics also sought to decentre the 'grand narrative' of class through the adoption of feminist principles in order to create space for different types of politics linked to new ideas about the nature of oppression, struggle and liberation. Importantly, sceptics argued that feminist ideas articulate a more authentic understanding and analysis of everyday life. Rather than trying to map a theory onto everyday experiences, as classical Marxism seeks to do, feminism uses everyday life as a theory in order to understand the position of women and other marginalised groups in society:

> The lived experience of class exploitation is not the only brand which socialism in the twentieth century must incorporate; it is not the only variant of exploitation which socialism must address... Other types of social experiences will have to be drawn on and build into socialism if it is to become a politics capable of fighting and transforming life on a variety of different 'fronts'. (Hall 1988, 181)

This rise of feminism and other movements provide alternative analyses of the nature of struggle and liberation and this feeds into the next element of the crisis: the rise of the post-industrial society and the decline in importance of the 'working class'. The combination of the rise of new social movements and the process of de-industrialisation helped to decentre the working class in terms of its importance as a political agent in socialist politics. As we have seen, socialist sceptics sought to decentre class in order to create space for new types of understandings of ordinary people. With the terminal decline of heavy industry and manufacturing sectors in Britain, the actual existing working class was slowly losing its organising principle as capital fled overseas in search of cheaper and less well organised labour (Amin 1994). The loss of employment and the realignment of capital from the production of tangible goods to the production of knowledge and services meant that the influence and power of a self-conscious working class was being radically altered. Socialists were seeking to build a new politics based on the recognition of the declining influence of the working class:

> This non-class encompasses all those who have been expelled from production by the abolition of work, or whose capacities are under-employed as a result of the industrialisation…of intellectual work…The majority of the population now belong to the post-industrial neo-proletariat…with no job security or definite class identity. (Gorz 1980, 68–9)

The final aspect of the crisis is the analysis of the threat of the New Right. Sim (2001, 4) discusses how many socialists were sceptical of the 'logic of history' to spark revolution and the downfall of capitalism. With the New Right appealing to populist sentiments and seeking to co-opt the public into consumption capitalism, sceptics wanted to reconstruct Marxist theory in order to make it more relevant to everyday people:

> There now seems little doubt that…the popular mood shifted decisively against the left…The right has re-established its monopoly over 'good ideas'; 'capitalism' and the 'free market' have come back into common usage as terms of positive approval. And yet the full dimension of this precipitation to the right still lack a proper analysis on the left…Our illusions remain intact, even when they clearly no longer provide an adequate analytic framework. (Hall 1988, 40)

Without renewal, sceptics warned, socialism would become irrelevant to ordinary people (Gorz 1980; Laclau and Mouffe 2001; Hall 1988).

This crisis in socialist politics leads to a crisis of confidence in the theory and practice of community development. Unlike the Structuralist discourse and some of its hard-line Marxist constructions I analysed in Chapter Three, community development discourses during this moment in time are forced to respond to the growing irrelevance of socialist politics and find a new path for theory and practice without relying exclusively on classical Marxism. The crisis of confidence for community development is based on the growing realisation that so-called 'radical practice' has been ineffective in influencing or countering macro-level structural issues that shape the lives of ordinary people:

> It seems inevitable that a community worker with a strong commitment to a Marxist position will experience tension between what he believes and what he does. His study of Marx will have informed him that people's lives are

> shaped by the economic system and the prevailing mode of production. In the field, however…a large part of his work is likely to be in connection with working class people's relationships to unhelpful institutions and large bureaucracies. (Salmon 1978, 82–3)

The crisis of confidence is also based on the realisation that radical practice has not politicised people to the socialist cause. In fact, at this moment, community development witnesses the exact opposite of its intentions – a rise in right-wing sentiments and in some extreme cases, fascist loyalties in some white working class communities:

> There are few accounts of successful community work achieving the radicalisation of a working class community and there is frequently some vagueness and uncertainty about the activities involved in such politicising efforts. Might this not demonstrate more than inadequate techniques but a mistaken analysis? (Lambert 1978, 11)

Thus in the context of a reconsideration of classical Marxism and the resulting crisis of confidence in community development, we can understand how the particular formation and structure of community development discourses take shape. Key texts that construct these discourses are drawn from two competing sources: the Association of Community Workers (ACW) and the National Institute for Social Services. The ACW, while a broad church, is mostly composed of 'radical' practitioners and theorists who have a historical or ideological connection to the CDPs. By radical, I mean the ACW membership was drawn from socialists, Marxist 'fellow-travellers', feminists and anti-racists and this diverse ideological range exemplify the texts of the post-Marxist discourse. The series of books edited and written by ACW from the mid-1970s to the mid-1980s represent an attempt to construct community development as radical and transformative (Mayo 1977; Wilson 1977; Curno 1978; Lambert 1978; Radford 1978; Salmon 1978; Smith 1978; Blagg and Derricourt 1982; Craig, Derricourt and Loney 1982; Dixon et al. 1982; Fleetwood and Lambert 1982; Filkin and Naish 1982). By the mid-1970s another competing discourse was emerging to challenge the ACW, however – this discourse is to be found in the series of texts published by National Institute for Social Services. Focusing primarily on the development of skills, expertise and practice theory for community development professionals these texts constitute the Realist discourse and remain some of the most popular and widely read community development texts today (Specht 1975; Henderson and Thomas 1980; Twelvetrees 1980; Henderson et al 1980).

I will now turn to analyse the post-Marxist and Realist discourses and identities further detail.

## The post-Marxist discourse: reconstructing radicalism?

The post-Marxist discourse is constituted by the texts, language and practices of community development practitioners and theorists seeking to build a new form of socialist theory and practice in order to better align the 'radical' rhetoric of community development with a clear practice base in neighbourhoods. I have named this discourse 'post-Marxist' because this category seems to best capture the project of reconstruction that constitutes this discourse during this moment in time. Buffeted by a crisis in Marxism, ineffective practice in communities and the popularity of the New Right in working class neighbourhoods, this discourse is uncertain and in flux but ultimately seeking to construct a reinvigorated form of radical professionalism in order to redistribute power and resources to marginalised groups.

It is important to recognize, however, that this new form of radicalism is born out of disillusionment with the dominant construction of radical socialist practice. The post-Marxist discourse should be viewed as an ambivalent inheritor of the Structuralist discourse of the CDPs. Recalling my analysis in Chapter Three, the Structuralist discourse was a two-pronged attempt to link urban poverty to capitalist development and demonstrate that the welfare state (and by extension community development) is part of the ideological state apparatus to dissipate revolutionary fervour among the working class. The post-Marxist discourse is seeking to subvert these key discursive practices and transform them. For example:

> In so far as many theoretical contributions don't lend themselves to translation into day-to-day objectives, I regard them as failures...This last point...seems particularly to dog the Marxist perspective with its holistic philosophy and concentration on production, both of which are hard (but not impossible) to relate to the localised and domestic context of community work...What worries me is that so far it has been the 'nihilistic' school which has exerted the greatest influence on fieldwork. Very probably, one reason for this is...its ability to offer a convenient 'explanation' for what most would agree has been a pretty uninspiring

performance from community work to date...Community work is portrayed as a means of social control and therefore doomed to fail the working class every time. (Smith 1978, 18–19)

I argue that the post-Marxist discourse is seeking to reconstruct three aspects of socialist community development: the state, the working class and the site and nature of community practice. I will discuss each of these ideas in turn. Here is a helpful summation of the discourse's attempt of reconstruction of its language and practices:

> We suggest that there is work to be done within the community that cannot be collapsed into the problems of industry that is specific to the structure and composition of the modern city and cannot be reduced to the 'class struggle' as it is commonly defined...Therefore community politics should go beyond struggles over traditional forms of class reproduction in the locality and engage seriously with those who perceive their oppressor not as the hidden hand of the market but as the very visible hand of the state (Blagg and Derricourt 1982, 17–20)

In seeking to reconstruct radicalism, I argue that the post-Marxist discourse first attempts to redefine the nature of the state. Rather than the state being a monolithic entity that seeks to manipulate, co-opt and suppress the working class in the interests of the ruling class – as argued by the Structuralist discourse – the state is instead constructed as multi-faceted, contradictory and malleable to the influence and interests of the working class. As Smith (1978, 21) argues:

> The state...is riddled with contradictions and hence contains possibilities for action. It contains...the seeds of its own future transformation; the form such transformation take will depend...on the means by which working class groups engage with the state.

As I argued in Chapter Three, for community development in the UK, the relationship with the state is perhaps the most important dynamic for practitioners – even more so than the relationship with community groups. Thus, it seems to me that for the post-Marxist discourse, rethinking the nature of the state is crucial for building new socialist community development practices. By rejecting the Structuralist discourse's dominant interpretation of the state as a tool for the ruling class, the post-Marxist discourse reassesses community development's role and purpose. Rather than constructing an antagonistic relationship with the state, the focus instead is on understanding and building a relationship with the *local* state in order to: take action on issues that are important to community groups; to make local services more accountable and accessible; and redistribute power in local decision-making (Smith 1978; Blagg and Derricourt 1982). This is an important transformation that the post-Marxist discourse attempts: the focus of community development practice should not be the theoretical 'state' of Marx, Gramsci or Althusser but the actual existing local state that people interact with on an everyday basis through social welfare services such as education, health and housing. This analysis of the local state is not new as it draws on the work of Cynthia Cockburn (1977), which I discussed in Chapter Three. What is new, however, is that Cockburn's analysis about the state seems to have moved into a mainstream position in community development. Here are two important articulations in the redefinition of the state:

> The particular savageness of Thatcherism has severely dented the credibility of one of the more cherished catechisms of the British Marxist primer, that capitalism 'needs' welfare... The state is not separate from us...rather it penetrates into every possible sphere of social relations, attempting to establish them as fields of its power...Both the parameters of the state and fields of its struggle are extended...The state has the task of organising those who have been ejected from the economic discourse. The elderly, the young and racial minorities...experience their exploitation...in officialdom, bureaucracy, isolation [and] indifference...such issues must be taken seriously. (Blagg and Derricourt 1982, 19–20)

This focus on the operation of the local state – its failures and opportunities for transformation – serve two purposes for the post-Marxist discourse: it captures the real lived experiences of ordinary people and it gives a meaningful, manageable and realistic scope of practice that community development can undertake. This new construction of the local state is emblematic of a new concept in the community development discursive repertoire during this moment in time: realism. As I demonstrated in Chapter Four in the American context, realism and pragmatism were used as a way to distance community development from radicalism. Through my analysis of the patterns in the language of texts in the UK context, it is clear that realism becomes the hook by which to construct a new form of radical professionalism: 'It does seem important to define a mode of community work which avoids utopianism…The focus for attention is not some alternative value system hard to imagine in real terms, but these commonly held values which bourgeois society fails to attain – greater equality, lessening poverty' (Lambert 1978, 14).

For the post-Marxist discourse, realism provides radicalism with a new meaning and focus. By having a more realistic depiction of the state and by constructing a new politics for engaging with the local state, the post-Marxist discourse is able to find a new impetus and legitimacy for radical practice. For example, here is pertinent example of realism as a new organising principle for radical practice:

> We have to function in the world of reality rather than in
> the world of ideas and dreams. In practice we are compelled
> to adjust to things as they really are. We have to lower our
> sights and go for that which is attainable. The real world
> is no world for the ideological purist. (Salmon 1978, 76)

This new and more realistic focus on the local state, local social welfare services and participation in local decision-making structures requires a new way of thinking about working class people and their interests. The next reconstruction the post-Marxist discourse undertakes is that of the 'working class'. I suggest that rather than using class as the foundational and totalising subject position by which to understand *all* experiences of local people, the discourse seeks to decentre class in order for it to sit alongside gender and to a lesser extent, race, as a means by which to capture more accurately the complex identities and interests of local people. We can see this decentring of class most clearly in the post-Marxist discourse's struggle to account for and accommodate the burgeoning second-wave feminist movement. Women's experiences and interests in the private sphere of community undermine the essentialising tendencies of the inherited Structuralist discourse in its constructions of the working class. As Wilson (1977, 4), a feminist critic of community development, observes:

> Community issues are indeed of central importance to
> women. The reality of community life, as opposed to the
> confused and romantic dream-image, is of women living
> in a direct relationship to the state as mediated through

housing departments, schools and the state welfare system which supports the family.

By decentring class, the post-Marxist discourse employs feminist principles in an attempt to construct a more realistic understanding of local people's lives and interests which in turn helps to re-legitimise radicalism in community development:

> If traditional forms of working class action are to be related to the new concerns of the [feminist] politics of personal life, we need to develop organisations capable of linking the two areas, of reconciling the personal and political... Community work has a role to play in...forging the links with feminism [and this] seems to me even more important than making links with the labour movement. (Smith 1978, 33–4)

Feminism's focus on the 'politics of everyday life' provides a way to link new ideas of the local state to a reconstituted 'working class'. Rather than defining, as the Structuralist discourse had done, working class experience through the lens of the workplace and the production of capital, the adoption of feminist principles allows the post-Marxist discourse to politicise the experiences of the collective consumption of social welfare in the private spheres of the home and community. The politics of everyday life re-legitimises neighbourhood work with local people who would not necessarily describe themselves or their interests as 'working class' but who do recognise that they occupy a marginalised and unequal position in society. As Blagg and Derricourt (1982, 20) argue:

> Political subjects, such as blacks, young people and women, who cannot be placed within the relations of production, come into prominence. Their position may be profoundly over-determined by class struggle but it is not simply reducible to it. It is necessary therefore that we perceive struggles and antagonisms within the community as possessing characteristics often different from class struggles and class antagonisms.

Indeed, feminism appears to provide the post-Marxist discourse with new articulations of democracy by attempting to create space for local people to define for themselves the terms of their oppression and liberation:

> We start with a person's own specific oppression because that experience is valuable in itself and it is most easy to identify with. The Women's Liberation Movement has taught us to see that process and goal are inseparable. We cannot achieve real liberating change...in a society by working in an oppressive manner; by doing so we will only replace one elite by [sic] another. (Dixon et al. 1982, 61)

The focus on the personal politics of women's and men's relationships to the local state in the form of the collective consumption of social welfare helps the post-Marxist discourse to reconstruct the final aspect of the Structuralist discourse – the purpose and practices of development work. Part of the ambivalent legacy of the Structuralist discourse is a focus on undermining capitalistic economic development. A consequence of that particular construction of community development was that many practitioners turned away from community-based work and focused instead on workplace and industrial struggles.

By focusing on the local state and by transforming the construction of the 'working class', the post-Marxist discourse is able to reconstruct radical practices away from the workplace to the defence and expansion of social welfare – especially in light of the Thatcher Government's retrenchment policies. The post-Marxist discourse ultimately seeks to construct community development as a process to support the transformation of the relationship between ordinary people and the local state: making the relationship less bureaucratic, less hierarchical and more democratic and accountable. In doing so, the post-Marxist discourse is seeking to make radicalism real and relevant to communities and make community development effective and legitimate in the eyes of ordinary people:

> Community workers operate in the domestic sphere. We usually work with the people for whom the promise of personal fulfilment has gone most sour. And we talk a lot about education and personal growth and development. Usually we talk about them in an embarrassed way as a second best to excuse our failure to stop the last rent rise. Maybe we ought to accept, willingly, that community work is partly about such things and to take them on in a more systematic way. (Smith 1978, 33)

In my view, however, this development of 'realistic radicalism' is problematic. Rather than rescuing radicalism from Marxist economic determinism and dogmatism, it appears to me that the post-Marxist discourse constitutes a capitulation of socialist ideas and practices. It is not clear how radical it is to defend the welfare state or connect people better to service provision. Indeed, it seems that was the entire point of the Home Office's Urban Programme and the CDPs in 1968, as I discussed in Chapter Three, which had no pretensions to radicalism. The question that remains regarding this discourse is why these rather pedestrian social democratic concepts and practices in relation to the state and the working class are being reconstructed as 'radical' within the post-Marxist discourse. My analysis of identity constructions may help to shed light on this question.

An ongoing problem in British community development identity constructions from 1968 onwards is that of the practitioner. As I analysed in Chapter Three, community development is preoccupied with the contradictory legitimacy of the practitioner being both a professional and a revolutionary. During this moment in time the practitioner is experiencing an identity crisis which is unsatisfactorily resolved. The post-Marxist discourse constitutes a break from the Structuralist discourse that constructs itself as a professional activist/ organic intellectual in aid of a revolution or at least in aid of a radical socialist movement for change. The post-Marxist practitioner is a contingent identity that is in the process of turning away from its former radical activist embodiment connected to trade unionism and socialist party politics, to a professional positioned within the local state and everyday community life. This 'becoming' professional is seeking legitimacy within the state and within communities. Here is an example of this ambivalence:

> After several years of debate, community work is still unable to face the transparent reality that it is a profession in all essentials. Professionalism implies limitations on practice, but far more limiting has been the stance of denying ourselves a professional status without saying, what, then, we are. The result has been a kind of collective identity crisis, which, I think accounts…for our lack of results. (Smith 1978, 32)

Because the discourse promotes the idea that only reformist and micro-level change is possible within the confines of a realistically radical community development practice, it inadvertently constructs 'legitimacy' in such a way as it must marginalise its former radical ideals. The identity crisis that constitutes the identity constructions of the discourse is the realisation that its former radical incarnation (as constituted by the Structuralist discourse) was misguided and ineffective and the post–Marxist professional is the only legitimate and available subject position during this politically salient moment.

With the post–Marxist professional disillusioned with classical Marxism and seeking to construct a stable (radical) identity, local people are once again constructed in contradictory terms. With the adoption of feminist and anti-racist discursive elements, local people in the post–Marxist discourse are starting to be recognised not as a homogeneous working class mass but as mass that is also gendered and racialised. With the recognition of issues relating to the sexual division of labour and institutional racism, 'the working class' is starting to break out of its reified state. It seems that one type of reification has been replaced with another, however. While it is the case that class has been decentred in relation to gender and race, 'women' and 'Blacks' are now treated as reified categories. For example, two texts about the 'Black community' and 'women' in community development essentialise these subject positions by assuming a unity of experience that may not necessarily exist for all women or all Black people (and as a consequence, erase Black women's experiences, who live at the intersection of race, class, gender and other identities). For example, here is a typical totalising use of race:

> A fundamental need of the black community in Britain is to be freed from the disabling effects of white racism both in the individual and institutional forms...The primary issue for the black community [is racism]. (Manning and Ohri 1982, 3)

Here is a fairly common example of how gender is essentialised:

> The problems women encounter at home and at work cannot be separated. They are part of the same process. ... Women get the worst rewarded and least interesting jobs... this situation is connected to women's role in the home. (Lawrence 1977, 12–3)

Despite these important transformations in the constituent nature of local people through the recognition of the existence of gender and race, a consistent pattern has started to emerge within British community development with regards to its construction of local people. Local people are still constructed as 'alienated' or 'bewildered' or 'in need' – in other words they remain a passive object to be acted on by the professional. Here is a typical example: 'Many people now need the help and guidance of a worker who can fathom the mysteries of the welfare state' (Lambert 1978, 11–12). Here is another example: 'The possibilities of revolutionary change are enhanced by the presence of a growing mass of people who are disaffected…but also incapacitated' (Smith 1978, 24). It is not clear to me how democratic or socially just it is for community development to construct local people as a passive homogenised object. As I have demonstrated in the previous chapters, by constructing local people as bewildered or disaffected this serves the purpose of legitimising the need for community development and community development professionals.

I will now turn to analyse the Realist discourse and its identity constructions.

## The Realist discourse: constructing a professional identity

The Realist discourse is constituted by the texts, language and practices of community development theorists and practitioners opposing the socialist discourse of community development and seeking to construct a renewed technocratic form of community development focused on skills and expertise in service provision and community engagement. The Realist discourse shares many discursive features with the post-Marxist discourse and as a result we can see an important synthesis between these two competing and ostensibly antagonistic discourses in terms of the construction and reproduction of a 'professional' identity. I have used the term 'Realist' to describe this discourse because this concept encapsulates the central claim of the discourse – that socialist community development practice is an unnecessary abstraction and misrepresentation of everyday life and only a focus on the production of 'practice theory' will make community development effective and relevant for the state, practitioners and ordinary people.

As with the post-Marxist discourse, my analysis suggests that the Realist discourse also seeks to reconstruct key ideas and practices of the inherited Structuralist discourse but not as a way to reform radical practice but to marginalise it. The Realist discourse attempts to marginalise and silence radicalism in community development by constructing a reformed profession and identity to demonstrate that community development is legitimate, viable and effective *without* socialist theories.

There are two important components of the Realistic discourse: the construction of radicalism as ineffective and the construction of an alternative 'non-ideological' form of professional practice. To begin, the Realist discourse constructs radical theory and practice as unrealistic, ineffective and irresponsible. In an influential text, Specht (1975, 22) argues:

> Community work, as an enterprise, is closer to a profession than a social movement…A social movement ideology will simply not provide community workers with the range of knowledge and skill required to carry out these tasks. If they function with a narrow ideology, community workers will face continuing disappointment and frustration and – in the long run – demonstrate incompetence.

This is an important pattern in the language of the discourse. Radicalism is not simply disagreeable or unnecessary; radicalism is constructed as a threat to effective community development practice. It is constructed as dangerous to good practice because it prevents practitioners from critically thinking about and developing a coherent set of skills that is directly relevant to everyday life in neighbourhoods. In other words, radicalism is all talk and no action, or worse still, radicalism is all rhetoric and irresponsible action:

> To the extent that the radical tendency offers no practice theory or practice paradigms, it is unprogressive [sic] and a political and professional distraction. At the very least, analyses without prescription for action are an extravagance both in a political movement and in a human services profession like community work. (Thomas 1978, 242)

In the Realist discourse, radicalism is characterised as a substitute for understanding and working in the real word. Rather than confronting reality, radicals choose to try to fit reality into their pre-determined worldview with disastrous results for community development. Thus for the Realist discourse, radicalism is constructed as both inauthentic and irrelevant because it fits ordinary people's diverse and divergent interests into a false category of homogeneous proletariat interests and actions:

> [Feminist] concerns with the politics of everyday life…help us see that the political analyses of the radical tendency in community work is cut off from the reality and experiences

of working class people…Not only is their [radicals] analysis divorced from practice but the analysis itself is detached from a patience and interest in the events and transactions of everyday working class life. (Thomas 1978, 24)

What is also interesting to note is how both the post-Marxist and the Realist discourses adopt feminism for their divergent purposes. Both discourses use feminist analyses of the 'politics of everyday life' in order to legitimise community development practice and infuse it with a sense of authenticity about its role and practices. For the Realist discourse, the invocation of feminism is used as a way to marginalise the idea of radicalism by branding it sexist. For example:

[There are] sexist elements in the ideology and motivations of the radical tendency…The concern to make and project community work as a radical alternative may be an expression of professional male machismo intent on distinguishing community work from (female) social work. (Thomas 1978, 24)

The irony of the Realist discourse invoking feminism is that while it certainly is the case that many women experienced sexism in socialist organisations, the Realist discourse does not seek to recognise or give voice to women subjects as its prime objective. Instead, feminism is used as a tool to undermine radicalism and in doing so, the Realist discourse also seeks to strip feminism of its radical implications by seeking to align it with its technocratic social practices.

By constructing radicalism as both ineffective and inauthentic, the Realist discourse is able to create space to construct a new professional identity and practices devoid of radicalism but steeped in expertise and technique:

[Community development is about] the structure and technical aspects of change…[such as] the systematic problem analysis that illuminate the various facets of the problem and identifies various subsystems and actors who play a part; the identification of programme goals, the building of organisations and communication systems, the design of programmes and of service delivery system and the skills for programme evaluation and review. (Specht 1975, 25)

The effectiveness and legitimacy of community development comes from a clear skills-set of building locally-based organisations, providing services, connecting people to those services and evaluating the impact of this work: 'The legitimacy of a profession has been said to lie in the acceptance of its claims to mastery of method (that is to say technology) not in its expertness in determining ends' (Waddington 1979, 234). By developing a coherent set of skills and techniques, the Realist discourse is able to rescue community development from its marginal position in both the state and in communities.

The discourse constructs the state in similar ways to the post-Marxist discourse. Rather than an impenetrable tool of the ruling class, the local state is constructed as unwieldy and bureaucratic – and open to influence. The role of the community development professional is to influence the workings of the state at the local level for the benefit of local people:

> One of the great social problems of our era is the problem of how to make large organisations function in ways that are humane, democratic and efficient…Community work has much to offer in finding new means to deal with the problems of large organizations. (Specht 1975, 23)

What is interesting to note at this point is the convergence between the Realist and post-Marxist discourses. Whether community development should be underpinned by socialist principles or whether it should be stripped of its perceived radicalism, community development still ends up being constructed as a profession whose primary role is to better connect the local state to ordinary people's interests. My analysis of the Realist discourse's identity constructions helps to demonstrate its similarity to the post-Marxist discourse.

Like the post-Marxist discourse, the Realist discourse constructs a 'becoming' professional whose uncertain and contingent role is to combine bureaucratic reform with community-based work in order to influence local services and support micro-level changes that benefit ordinary people:

> Community workers are aligned with the people by identification and principles but they are employed on the whole by local and central state agencies. Community workers stand…between the world of welfare professionals in which they gain the means to live and the movement for change to which they belong. They are in the welfare

> state but not of it but they are also in community groups but seldom, if ever, of them. (Henderson, Jones and Thomas 1980, 6)

Unlike the post-Marxist discourse, the Realist discourse does not construct this 'becoming' professional identity as a moment of crisis, but as the above quote demonstrates, the Realist discourse recognises the contradictory space in which the professional operates. Because the Realist discourse seeks to locate the professional in this contradictory and marginal space between the state and community, this problematic site of community development provides further impetus for the need to develop a pragmatic and expert identity and abandon the distractions of radicalism in order to legitimise and stabilise community development.

Constructions of local people in this discourse also share discursive similarities to the post-Marxist discourse. Part of the Realist discourse's attempt to marginalise radicalism is that the professional will be better able to understand the interests and needs of local people by abandoning Marxist dogma. Once again I have identified a problem with the treatment of local people, however – they are constructed as passive objects. As with the post-Marxist discourse, because the Realist discourse is preoccupied with questions of legitimacy of its professional identity, the discourse fails to construct local people based on equality and justice. Local people are a homogenised mass requiring the active professional for support and guidance. For example:

> Community work is concerned with participation and with a spirit and methods of working that include people…It seeks to enable marginal groups to migrate into the 'acting community' of decisions and decision-making. (Henderson, Jones and Thomas 1980, 5)

Earlier I noted how the Realist discourse uses feminist principles as a means to marginalise the post-Marxist discourse. The Realist discourse however does not seek to recognise or construct a sense of local people as racialised, gendered or classed. Frequently the only time local people are referred to is to undermine the competing post-Marxist discourse:

> The poor and deprived, do, frequently, feel poor and deprived. But I am not sure that they feel the sense of apathy, hopelessness and despair that is expressed [by socialists] in

describing the difficulties of community work. (Specht 1975, 23)

By emphasising realism and the construction of a legitimate professional identity, it seems, perhaps surprisingly, that the Realist and post-Marxist discourses share similar practices of constructing local people in unequal and disrespectful ways. Rather than being recognised as active subjects, local people are homogenised and assumed to be passive. This construction re-enforces the need for a legitimate, active and professional community development worker.

## Conclusions

In this chapter I have argued that the 1979–1985 politically salient moment constitutes a time of crisis and transformation in the micropolitics of British community development. The crisis in socialist politics signals an even deeper identity crisis for community development. With the shift away from key ideas of Marxism including that of the 'working class', the 'logic of history' and the repressive nature of the state, community development finds itself adrift. With the realisation that radical practice can be both dogmatic and ineffective, various community development discourses are prompted to respond and attempt reconstructions of its identities and practices. I have demonstrated the surprisingly similar ways in which the post-Marxist and Realist discourses respond to this moment. Rather than being in conflict with each other, the discourses converge in both their construction of the problem of radicalism and in the construction of possible solutions. In the end and for different reasons, each discourse characterises professionalism as the solution to the crisis of Marxism and the ineffectiveness of radical community practice. What is interesting to note is how the constituent nature of that professionalism and the professional identity of the community development practitioner are similar in the ostensibly antagonistic post-Marxist and Realist discourses.

Professionalism seems to be a shorthand for pragmatism and lower expectations about what community development can actually achieve in a hostile and uncertain political environment. A commitment to working at the grassroots is constructed in each of the discourses as a commitment to rather modest practices: connecting ordinary people better to the local state. In many ways, the discourses' construction of professionalism appears to regress to the Rationalist discourse of the Home Office and the Gulbenkian Foundation that I analysed in

Chapter Three. Democratising the local state is, of course, a laudable aim for community development. The issue for me, however, is why this shift to modest and pedestrian goals is characterised in the post-Marxist discourse as 'radical' and in the Realist discourse as 'innovative' especially given the fact that local people are still being constructed as passive objects requiring the leadership of professionals.

As we move into the final political moment – the convergence of Left/Right politics in the 1990s – it is important to keep in mind several points regarding the micropolitics of community development in both America and Britain. First, from 1968 onwards, it has become apparent that the majority of community development discourses fail to construct identities for community development professionals and local people based on equality and respect. Regardless of the political philosophy that informs the discourses, this is a consistent pattern across the language and texts of both the American and British discourses. Related to this, the opportunity for an oppositional discourse to develop which challenges these dominant identity constructions appears to hinge on the discourses' relationship to and adoption of ideas linked to participatory democracy and anti-racist feminisms.

In Britain, in the context of a strong welfare state and relatively popular social democratic politics, no discourse has yet developed that seeks to construct non-hierarchical relationships between professionals and local people. I think this is because the micropolitics of British community development are all orientated towards the state. Because the state occupies a central role in British community development, the professional is perpetually trying to find a place for itself within its structures. The professional is not in control of her identity and is made contingent by her relationship to the welfare state. By trying to construct the professional as competent and legitimate, this dominates the formation, structure and operation of the various discourses – regardless of political leanings. As a result of the focus on professionalism, this leads to local people being constructed in problematic ways. In order to reinforce the legitimacy of a professional identity, local people must be constructed as a passive object to be acted on by the professional. This particular construction of local people creates a perpetual need for the professional and reinforces the legitimacy of the professional within state structures.

In terms of the micropolitics in America, we can see how a comparatively weak welfare state and a marginal tradition of socialist politics influence the formation and structure of these community development discourses. The discourses draw on a greater variety of political philosophies to inform their language and they are not primarily focused on arguing for their legitimacy and professional status in relation to the state. The focus here is about atomised and autonomous neighbourhood change. This, of course, creates its own problems in terms of not having a clear analysis about the relationship between the state, the market and civil society. Regardless, American community development is also not able to consistently construct equal and respectful identities between professionals and local people. As I have demonstrated, the vast majority of discourses in the US fail to generate non-hierarchical identity constructions and based on my analysis I think this is because local people need to be defined as a passive object in order to provide a justification for the revolutionary, populist or technical fervour of the respective professional. It is important to note, however, that it has only been in the American tradition that discourses have developed which seek to subvert these dominant constructions. The weakness of the state in the US has created spaces for alternative community development practices. Drawing on ideas of participatory democracy, feminism and anti-racism these oppositional discourses subvert the dominant identity constructions in order to develop new community development identities and practices based on radical democratic principles. It is in the potential of these marginal discourses that I think community development can be reconstructed and reoriented towards democracy, equality and social justice.

As I turn now to examine the final politically salient moment, it will be important to consider whether the trends I have identified are reproduced or challenged in America and Britain.

# CHAPTER SIX

# Commodifying community: American community development and neoliberal hegemony

## Introduction

In the last two chapters I analysed the micropolitics of American and British community development during the 1970s and 1980s and demonstrated how, more often than not, community development produces and reproduces problematic language, social practices and identities that seem to undermine the practice of equality and social justice for marginalised groups. In response to the growing dominance of the New Right, American community development sought accommodation within an emerging neoliberal politics focused on valourising the individual, the free market and shrinking the welfare state. British community development, in response to a crisis in socialist politics, pursued a more technocratic path focused on strengthening the professionalism of the field in order to win legitimacy with the state and local people. The one exception to these dominant practices is the Empowerment discourse which is constituted by the ideas and social practices of anti-racist feminism. As a successor to the Democracy discourse, which I analysed in Chapter Two, the Empowerment discourse is the only discourse I identified that constructs its politics and relational identities for practitioners and local people based on equality and respect during that moment. This is important because it strongly suggests that the language and social practices of anti-racist feminism are central to helping community development to fulfil its claims about supporting the social justice claims and self-determination for local people.

This chapter focuses on the micropolitics of community development from 1992 to 1997 in the United States. I have identified two discourses for analysis. The 'Revitalisation discourse' is constituted by the texts, language and practices of official state actors in President Bill Clinton's Administration and practitioners working in community economic development seeking to build social, political and economic capital in poor communities in order to transform a so-called 'underclass' into an emergent capitalist class focused on enterprise and entrepreneurship. For the Revitalisation discourse, community development is constructed as a tool to convey the principles of neoliberalism and thus reconcile poor people to the new economic reality of limited state support and the importance of self-reliance. In opposition to these practices, the 'Coalition discourse' is constituted by the texts, language and practices of feminist, anti-racist and Alinskyist practitioners seeking to build grassroots-based alliances across differences in identity in order to oppose the hegemonic practices of the New Right and promote progressive social change. For the Coalition discourse, community development is constructed as a process for building and strengthening a civil society composed of empowered citizens. As I shall demonstrate, these discourses emerge in response to two important events: the hegemony of the New Right coalition which forced the Democratic Party to shift to the right in order to become more appealing to voters and the divisiveness of so-called 'identity politics' which fractured left-wing politics throughout the late 1980s and 1990s.

## The new Democrats in a post-Reagan America

> The Reagan revolution did succeed where it mattered most – redirecting federal fiscal and economic policies – and the impact on low-income communities was devastating. In addition to the withdrawal of federal aid, the communities suffered from increased income inequality, capital flight, labour setbacks and crippling budgeting deficits...The very idea of community development policy...was challenged by a harsh, individualistic ideology positing that no intervention [in poor communities] would work. (O'Connor 1998, 114)

When Bill Clinton won the presidential election in 1992, his road to success was made possible by the political philosophy and policy priorities of the 'New Democrats'. The New Democrats were a response to the popularity of the New Right philosophy of the Republican Party and the disastrous election defeats that had become all too common for the Democrats since Reagan's landslide victory in 1980. As I discussed in Chapter Four, the New Right is a coalition of social and fiscal conservatives bound together by shared beliefs in radical individualism, free market capitalism and a limited state. With rising levels of economic inequality in the US due to the globalisation of capital, however, voters were looking for an innovative government response that would protect individuals and businesses from the worst effects of unbridled market forces but also preserve 'traditional American values' of individualism and self-reliance (for a more detailed discussion of this see: Clinton 2004; From 2005; Katz 2008). After eight years under Reagan and four years under President George H.W. Bush, it was clear that a continuation of New Right Republican policies would not provide middle and working class voters with effective protection from globalisation and the subsequent flight of capital and jobs overseas. Traditional Democratic redistributionist 'tax and spend' policies remained deeply unpopular, however. Thus the New Democrats identified an opportunity to develop a new type of politics that would serve the twin purposes of reconciling social democracy and neoliberalism while simultaneously repositioning the Democratic Party to make it more appealing to voters. Here is Robert Philpot (1999, 1), one of the architects of the New Democrats, reflecting on this merger of left and right politics:

> The New Democrat movement emerged in the early 1990s from the realisation that...the old ideologies of liberalism and conservatism were increasingly frustrating voters because of the false choices these imposed...New Democrats have promoted the notion of a new social contract between the state and the individual, arguing that the left's traditional concern for promoting opportunity needs to be married with a greater sensitivity to the responsibilities that citizens have towards the community.

Heavily influenced by the emerging Communitarian agenda of Putnam (1995) and Etzioni (1993), the New Democrats were seeking a compromise between social democracy and neoliberalism by promoting equality of opportunity *through* free market capitalism as the way for all groups, regardless of race or class, to achieve prosperity. The Democrat Leadership Council (DLC), an internal Democratic Party grouping which represented the New Democrats' policy platform, defined their compromise between left and right as such:

> We believe the promise of America is equal opportunity, not equal outcome...We believe that economic growth is the prerequisite to expanding opportunity for everyone. The free market, regulated in the public interest, is the best engine of general prosperity...We believe the purpose of social welfare is to bring the poor into the nation's economic mainstream, not to maintain them in dependence...We

believe that American citizenship entails responsibility as
well as rights. (DLC 1990 quoted in From 2005, 3–4)

For the New Democrat Clinton Administration, 'democratic capitalism'
and the 'opportunity agenda' were promoted as the most effective way
to tackle persistent poverty and address poor people's dependency on
the welfare state (Clinton 2004, 1–2). By seeking to boost economic
output while at the same time equipping people with the necessary
skills to compete effectively in the globalised free market, the New
Democrats maintained their commitment to equality but appended
ideas of competition, privatisation, individualism and self-reliance to
it. Furthermore, and as an added bonus, they did not need to pursue
unfashionable policies of expanding social welfare. Indeed to achieve
this 'third way' the Clinton Administration could, in the name of
equality, shrink the state by divesting it of responsibility for the social
and economic outcomes of the public. As Clinton (2004, 2) argued:
'In their heart of hearts, most Americans know that the best social
programme is a job'.

For community development, the New Democrats' 'opportunity
agenda' was implemented via Clinton's urban policy programme.
Clinton, in a 'new covenant' with cities, aimed to regenerate poor
inner-city areas through his flagship urban initiative, Empowerment
Zones/Enterprise Communities (EZ/EC). The EZ/EC attempted to:

> move beyond a focus on countercyclical grant-in-aid
> programs to an emphasis on enabling cities to compete
> in the global economy...[by fostering] locally initiated,
> bottom-up strategies that connect the public, business and
> neighbourhood sectors in community-building partnerships
> for change. (O'Connor 1998, 115–6)

Under this programme, cities would get targeted funding for regeneration
through the creation of designated zones that would offer tax-breaks
to promote private sector investment. Within these zones, new types of
'comprehensive' community initiatives (CCIs) were promoted: through
public–private partnerships, community development corporations
(CDCs) would get funding to rebuild the local economy by training
residents in entrepreneurial skills, building affordable housing and
delivering social welfare services (O'Connor 1998, 115–7; Katz 2008,
127–9). This is an important break with Democrats' progressive past.
Rather than the federal government directly intervening to tackle
persistent urban problems such as unemployment, poverty, crime and

poor housing, the Clinton Administration chose instead to transfer responsibility for these problems to the private and non-profit sectors through CDCs and CCIs. Clinton effectively privatised urban social problems.

The EZ/EC programmes 'have a tough-minded, economic growth-oriented...aura of promoting the work ethic as a solution to poverty' (Lemann 1995, 4). With Clinton's concern to be seen as 'pro-growth' and not 'pro-government', we can see how the Revitalisation discourse is formed and structured. Texts which constitute the Revitalisation discourse include those in relation to the EZ/EC programme of the Clinton Administration and those concerned with community economic development and building social and economic capital in poor neighbourhoods (Lemann 1995; Zdenek 1994; Putnam 1995; Rubin 1997; Gittell and Vidal 1998; Ferguson and Dickens 1999; O'Connor 1998; Katz 2008).

In addition to promoting their pro-growth agenda, the New Democrats were also concerned with building a 'new' New Deal coalition as an effective counterweight to the formidable alliance of the New Right. As From (2005, 2), a proponent of the New Democrat philosophy, argues:

> As the 1960s passed into the 1970s, the liberal agenda... ran out of steam, and the intellectual coherence of the New Deal began to dissipate. The Democratic coalition split apart over civil rights, Vietnam, economic change, and culture and values and the great causes of liberal government that had animated the Democratic Party for three decades degenerated into a collection of special pleaders.

Standing in the way of this big tent coalition of liberals, the New Democrats argued, were those 'special pleaders' engaging in divisive 'identity politics' based on the recognition of difference in terms of race, class, gender, sexuality and disability. As Todd Gitlin (1995, 84), a founder of Students for a Democratic Society and a prominent left-wing critic of identity politics argued:

> Between Left and Right there has taken place a curious reversal. The Left believed in a common human condition, the Right in fundamental differences among classes, nations, races...Today it is the Right that speaks a language of commonalities. Its rhetoric of global markets and global freedoms has something of the old universalist ring. To be

on the Left, meanwhile, is to doubt that one can speak of humanity at all.

During this moment, identity politics had come to be seen by the New Democrats as a chauvinistic distraction which allowed the Right to solidify its political power and shape popular public opinion (for a detailed discussion of this see: Gitlin 1995; for a dissenting view see: Hill Collins 2000).

Not all progressives defined 'identity politics' as a problem, however. Instead, the 'recognition of difference' was seen as an essential process for achieving social justice and democracy for marginalised groups. Here is Iris Marion Young (1990, 4–5) in her influential discussion about recognition as a political right:

> In the past, group-conscious policies were used to separate those defined as different and exclude them from access to the rights and privileges enjoyed by dominant groups. A crucial principle of democratic cultural pluralism...is that group-specific rights and policies should stand together with general civic and political rights of participation and inclusion.

In addition to difference being a political and social right for marginalised groups, difference could be used as a catalyst to build alliances and coalitions that could effectively counter the big tent politics of the New Right. Here is Nancy Fraser (1997, 10) in her influential text about the need to combine recognition and redistribution struggles in order to build an effective politics for social justice:

> The intersection of class, 'race', gender, and sexuality intensifies the need for transformative solutions, making the combination of socialism and deconstruction more attractive still...That combination best promotes coalition building is especially pressing today, given the multiplication of social antagonisms, the fissuring of social movements, and the growing appeal of the Right in the United States. In this context, the project of transforming the deep structures of both political economy and culture appears to be the one overarching programmatic orientation capable of doing justice to all current struggles against injustice.

Thus we can see the Coalition discourse take shape from these broader debates about multiculturalism, identity politics and the process of building solidarity across different social groups. Rather than dismiss identity politics, the Coalition discourse seeks to recognise and legitimise the discrete claims-making of different groups and use difference as a way to forge common bonds across competing identities and interests in order to build a new progressive alliance for social change. Texts which constitute the Coalition discourse include those in relation to feminist, anti-racist and Alinksyist community development practice seeking build multi-racial and multi-class alliances for social justice (Rubin and Rubin 1992; Bradshaw, Soifer and Gutierrez 1994; Daley and Wong 1994; Gutierrez and Lewis 1994; Mondros and Wilson 1994; Rosenthal and Mizrahi 1994; Miller, Rein and Levitt 1995; Delgado 1998; Fabricant and Burghardt 1998; Fisher and Shragge 2000).

## The Revitalisation discourse: recapitalising communities

The Revitalisation discourse should be seen as an inheritor of two previous discourses: the 1968 Poverty discourse and the 1979 Partnership discourse which I analysed in Chapters Two and Four. Those two discourses were constituted by official state actors and technocrats focused on using professional knowledge and expertise to resolve social problems. As I will demonstrate, the Revitalisation discourse reproduces these linguistic patterns and social practices. Two interrelated concepts structure the Revitalisation discourse: 'community-building' and 'empowerment'; I will discuss each of these ideas in turn.

First and most important, the Revitalisation discourse constructs 'community' as a privatised and marketised space. Communities are geographically defined neighbourhoods that are also emerging markets for capital investment. Thus a key practice of this discourse is to marketise communities: neighbourhoods are primarily constructed as places where the local economy has collapsed and partnerships between the state, corporations and local people are needed to jumpstart economic growth. For the Revitalisation discourse, communities are indistinguishable from any other free market in which a variety of goods and services can be bought, sold or traded for profit. Once 'community' is constructed as a market, the discourse then defines all relationships at the neighbourhood level (between local people, professionals, the state and the non-profit and private sectors) in terms of the marketplace – hence the pattern in the language of the discourse relating to social, political and economic capital. Indeed, as an official working on the

Clinton Administration's flagship urban policy of Empowerment Zones and Enterprise Communities (EZ/EC) put it:

> There is real money to be made in these markets...The goal here is...to make companies take a second look in our own backyard where there could be profitable business opportunities while also helping rebuild communities that have been left behind [in terms of economic prosperity]. (Sperling 1999 quoted in Katz 2008, 129)

Consequently, 'community-building' in the Revitalisation discourse is constructed as the process of recapitalisation of neighbourhoods: transforming communities from failed markets into competitive marketplaces to be exploited for profit by local people and private businesses. Communities are constructed as 'untapped areas for potential investment...undiscovered territories for many businesses' the goal of communities is to 'inspire private companies to build plants and stores in areas that the economic boom has largely passed by' (Clinton 1999 quoted in Katz 2008, 129). With capital flight defined as the key problem facing poor inner-city communities, community development is constructed as a primarily economic regeneration activity of making poor communities more attractive investment opportunities for private-sector enterprises and building the asset base of poor people:

> Community development produces assets that improve the quality of life for neighbourhood residents. Although ownership and control of these assets might be preferred, increasing access [to assets] is also important because it too expands opportunity. (Ferguson and Dickens 1999, 4)

What I find interesting about the Revitalisation discourse are the patterns in the language that echo the broader neoliberal discourse of the New Right. This is an important development in the discourse of community development. Unlike the Partnership discourse in Chapter Four, there does not seem to be any ambivalence about the wholesale adoption of the New Right politics in the Revitalisation discourse. The adoption of neoliberalism by this discourse is treated as innovative, obvious and commonsense.

Effective community-building takes place when the social, economic and political wealth and assets are recapitalised in a given neighbourhood:

Economic development is a process and approach used to create jobs, assets and an investment climate in distressed neighbourhoods and cannot be separated from community development...The key to a comprehensive, coordinated and integrated approach to community development is...maximising the commitment, capacity and efforts of neighbourhood residents and institutions...[and] increasing public and private capital investments in neighbourhoods. (Zdenek 1994, 6)

Thus for the Revitalisation discourse, the concept of 'empowerment' is intertwined with notions of the free market: empowerment is generated when local people begin to define themselves not as citizens but as capitalists searching for profit. Community-building supports empowerment by giving people a financial stake in their marketised communities. As Rubin (1997, 87–8) argues:

Empowerment occurs both for [community development organisations] and for individuals through material ownership of goods, property and social and job skills. Through such ownership individuals gain confidence to fight for more for themselves and for the broader community.

Capitalism empowers people by encouraging and supporting poor people's participation in marketised relationships. By becoming a homeowner or an entrepreneur, poor people and their communities can, for the first time, benefit from rather than be the victims of the wealth-generating power of free markets:

To create empowerment requires people to have ownership of material things as well as owning psychologically a better sense of self...Empowerment occurs as people who have been excluded learn that their efforts pay off in material advantages for themselves and their communities... Empowerment through ownership benefits the broader community through strategies to circulate wealth within communities of need. (Rubin 1997, 81–2)

By inculcating people with the concepts and practices of capitalism, community development is supporting poor people's self-reliance and reconciling poor people to the realities of limited state support and the challenges of operating in a context dominated by the free market. As one commentator has recently suggested:

> Only tough medicine would induce recovery [in poor neighbourhoods]. The cold bath of the market, painful (even fatal) to many in the short run…eventually would produce a solid and lasting prosperity that would diffuse work and good wages among the entire population…This was…a necessary discipline…The new urban strategies offered the urban poor their only long-range hope. (Katz 2008, 136)

Finally, in the context of neoliberal hegemony, empowerment is defined as being realistic about the limited resources that are now available for community development activities and shifting the responsibility of social welfare from the state to local people. Given this context, it is no surprise that 'asset-based community development' – the movement within the field of community development that seeks to reorient theory and practice from community needs, deficits and problems to a focus on community skills, strengths and power – comes to prominence:

> The hard truth is that development must start from within the community and, in most of our urban neighbourhoods, there is no other choice. Creative neighbourhood leaders across the country have begun to recognize this hard truth, and have shifted their practices accordingly. They are discovering that wherever there are effective community development efforts, those efforts are based upon an understanding, or map, of the community's assets, capacities and abilities…The key to neighbourhood regeneration, then, is to locate all of the available local assets, to begin connecting them with one another in ways that multiply their power and effectiveness, and to begin harnessing those local institutions that are not yet available for local development purposes. (Kretzmann and McKnight 1993, 3–4)

As I pointed out earlier, the identities that the Revitalisation discourse constitute are very similar to that of the Poverty discourse in Chapter Two and the Partnership discourse in Chapter Four. Unsurprisingly given the emphasis in this discourse on the free market, the community development practitioner is constructed as an expert reformer who brings entrepreneurial spirit and skills to the failed markets that are poor neighbourhoods. By coordinating large urban regeneration projects such as affordable housing through organisations such as community development corporations (CDCs) or comprehensive community initiatives (CCIs), this expert reformer is also invested with agency:

> [Professionals] need the patience and forbearance of community organisers with the business acumen of a free-booting, entrepreneurial capitalist…The work of development activists [is of] mastering skills in social administration – in budgeting, personnel management, negotiations…It is through skills in these technical matters that community-based development organisations are enabled to do the projects that renew hope and empower those within poor communities. (Rubin 1997, 86)

This reformer is focused on building the economic assets of poor people and poor neighbourhoods. As I have consistently charted throughout this book, the expert reformer is constructed as a subject who acts on contradictorily constructed local people. Similar to what I have demonstrated in my last four chapters, local people in the Revitalisation discourse are characterised as passive and disorganised objects requiring the intervention of the reformer. In particular, local people are constructed as lacking social capital – strong bonds with their neighbours – and thus need to be organised to build mutual trust and reciprocity before the neighbourhood can be successfully converted into a functioning marketplace:

> Increasing social capital where it is currently lacking is a challenging undertaking…The targeted areas have suffered from years of decline and neglect. In many of these neighbourhoods, the most successful and competent individuals and businesses move out when they can, often leaving social and economic vacuums…These neighbourhoods tend to have high rates of crime and violence that generate low levels of trust and cooperation among residents…This context makes it quite difficult to build strong bonds among residents and to build new bridges to the support community. (Gittell and Vidal 1998, 22)

Local people are also constructed as latent capitalists needing the skills and guidance of the professional to build capacity, however:

> Learning business skills in a supportive environment
> empowers community members. People are able to form
> their own enterprises as the community-based development
> organisation can buffer them during periods of low business
> growth...The goal of the community-based development
> organisation is to help community members overcome the
> disadvantages society has placed on them because they are
> poor and minority. (Rubin 1997, 70)

As I have argued in Chapters Two and Five with regard to the
Power, Poverty and Structuralist discourses, when local people
are simultaneously constructed as both passive objects and latent
subjects, it is not clear how the discourse is able to reconcile this
problematic construction. If the poor are passive and disorganised, as
the Revitalisation discourse defines them to be, it is difficult to see
how they also possess the capacity to be entrepreneurs. It is only when
the reformer acts on the poor to transform them from passive objects
to emerging capitalist subjects that this problematic identity can be
somewhat reconciled. As I have continually argued throughout this
book, I am not convinced about how this hierarchical relationship
between professionals and local people supports the goals of equality
and social justice that community development espouses.

Rather than community development providing an alternative
language and social practice for understanding community life and
practising social justice, it appears that community development
entrenches and expands the domination of already marginalised groups.

I will now turn to analyse the Coalition discourse.

## The Coalition discourse: unity through diversity

The Coalition discourse is constituted by the texts, language and
practices of feminist, anti-racist and Alinskyist community organisers
and practitioners seeking to build popular community-based alliances
based on difference to oppose the New Right and promote progressive
social change. Here are Miller, Rein and Levitt (1995, 115–6)
articulating the key ideas of the discourse:

> Organising around identity seeks to break conventional
> ways of 'conducting business' by reframing issues along new
> principles of justice or equality...This does not reflect left–
> right ideological splits but conveys a democratic ideology
> which transcends traditional political dichotomies. The goal

is transformational change, not only specific improvements in community or nation.

The Coalition discourse appears to be an amalgamation of the Empowerment and Populist discourses which I analysed in Chapter Four. The Empowerment discourse's key practice was to recognise difference in terms of gender and race in community organisations while the Populist discourse's key practice was building popular grassroots organisations to unite poor and working class people based on class affinities. The Coalition discourse combines elements of the Populist and Empowerment discursive practices in order to articulate a new discourse concerned with building popular grassroots-based organisations that recognise difference. As I previously discussed, given the divisions on the left due to rise of identity politics, the Coalition discourse is seeking to reconcile the competing claims-making between different identity and issue based groups by building alliances which unite rather than fracture left-wing interests. For instance, here is Gary Delgado (1998, 3), an influential community development author and activist, attempting to amalgamate 'recognition and redistribution' interests for the purposes of coalition building:'if traditional community organising is to become a force for change…it must proactively address issues of race, class, gender, corporate concentration and the complexities of a trans-national economy'.

Indeed, due to the hegemony of the New Right, broad-based alliances that mirror and effectively counter right-wing coalitions are a central feature of this discourse. As Mondros and Wilson (1994, 250) argue:

> The absence of coalitions hampers the ability to work across issues, to develop local constituencies for national campaigns and to connect local grievances with the national agenda… There must be attempts to bring middle-class and low-income organisations together around common cause. There is nothing more innately incompatible about this coalition than there is about upper-class businessmen and working-class fundamentalists being part of the Republican Party.

As with the Revitalisation discourse, the same interrelated concepts structure the Coalition discourse: 'community-building' and 'empowerment'. For the Coalition discourse, however, the concept of community-building is the way to redefine the nature and purpose of community. Rather than constructing community as a consensual geographical space with a homogeneous identity (as the Revitalisation discourse does), the Coalition discourse constructs 'community' as a space that reflects multiple interests, identities, concerns and conflicts. Community is a space that people occupy that is their own – it is not mediated by the state or the market. Instead, community is a 'free space', a network of individuals and groups with multiple and competing interests and identities:

> Empowered communities are built up from liberated networks in which people are willing to work together because they share multiple overlapping interests and not simply a geographic or an ethnic affinity. Future organising should portray community as a shared environment rich with the possibility for progressive groups to build on each others' success...An important step in forging a broad-based progressive movement is to bring disparate interests into this rich community of cooperation. (Rubin and Rubin 1992, 446)

For the Coalition discourse, the foundation for effective community-building begins with recognising difference. This discourse constructs community as the site of difference and thus the task of community-building is the search for common cause which unites the different identities and claims-making among local people. As advocates of alliances, Rosenthal and Mizrahi (1994, 10–11) state:

> We believe community-based organisations have a greater impact on issues by joining forces and building coalitions... Local issues usually represent larger patterns: social and economic problems that affect individuals and communities are often intertwined and compounded...Structured correctly, coalitions are open and egalitarian...They are also viable multicultural efforts that integrate minority and majority groups, new immigrants and more settled residents and traditionally powerless groups and those more powerful.

The Coalition discourse appears to be interpellating Mills' (1963) sociological imagination whereby private troubles are transformed into public issues. By recognising and acknowledging difference in terms of identity and interests and then by using the idea of difference to help build popular alliances that are composed of a broad range of constituents, the Coalition discourse is seeking to equate community-building with the construction of a democratic civil society:

> Just as individuals gain power by joining together, many small, alternative progressive organisations collectively working on a common problem can bring about large change…Activists must overcome the divisive tensions within the progressive movement and share a common vision and mutual respect. (Rubin and Rubin 1992, 457)

For the Coalition discourse, community development is constructed as the process by which to support community-building in terms of encouraging an organised and democratic left-wing voice that speaks to both the discrete interests and the common private troubles of different groups. By building alliances based on difference, the Coalition discourse is constructing ways in which a diverse range of individuals and groups can struggle together for expanded social, political and economic rights – transforming those common private troubles into public issues. Ultimately, community-building is characterised as a way in which community-based problems can be linked to and explained by the social, political and economic structures of American society which reproduce inequalities. Here are Fabricant and Burghardt (1998, 56–7) discussing the connection between these micro and macro level issues:

> Only by offering a straight-forward economic explanation of this decline [of inner-city neighbourhoods] can a national conversation reopen regarding a redistributive welfare state and the potential to join races, genders and classes…in one common purpose…Progressives must see, as the right saw after the 1964 Presidential election [in which Barry Goldwater was defeated], that only by fighting for a clear economic and social vision can power be re-attained to create genuine redistributive legislation.

The concept of empowerment is inter-related to the process of community-building. Since a key practice of the Coalition discourse is to unite local people across difference and build a progressive alliance as a counterweight to the New Right, the discourse constructs the process by which people organise themselves to redefine private troubles as public issues as empowerment. For the Coalition discourse, empowerment is constructed as a group's sense of its own efficacy. This efficacy is crucial for people to recognise their common cause and for people to link micro-level social problems to the particular ways in which social, economic and political institutions are organised:

> People want not only power but to feel empowered...These people feel bypassed in our society...They are made to feel small and insignificant in all their dealings with government and corporate bureaucracies...Social action organisations are places where they feel competent, capable, in charge and they can act on those feelings. (Mondros and Wilson 1994, 244)

Empowerment is both the product and a key driver of community-building. By uniting and organising, local people experience a sense of agency and efficacy. This agency and efficacy is then reinforced through building solidarity and reciprocity in the context of a community composed of difference. As Rosenthal and Mizrahi (1994, 13) explain:

> Coalitions allow groups to pursue bigger targets on a larger scale, address power inequities, [and] shape public ideology...Bridging differences, coalitions can help diverse groups develop a common language and ideology with which to shape a collective vision for social change.

The Coalition discourse constructs identities for professionals and local people that oppose the dominant model reproduced by the majority of community development discourses I have analysed in this book. Rather than constitute a hierarchical binary identity whereby the professional is an active subject and local people are passive objects, the Coalition discourse instead creates identities that are very similar to those of the Democracy and Empowerment discourses that I analysed in Chapters Two and Four. First, the Coalition discourse defines the professional as a 'facilitator of difference'. Several texts that constitute this discourse are concerned with mediating and reconciling the reality of competing and conflicting interests and identities within and between local people. As a facilitator, the professional is interested in using the free space of community as a site for deliberation and dialogue in order to bridge difference. For example:

> The organiser must approach the community as a facilitator...The organiser [should] take a collaborative approach, promoting democracy, participatory processes in the organising effort. This element is important

in empowering individuals... and serves to diminish
divisiveness and promote coalition-building between
groups. (Bradshaw, Soifer and Gutierrez 1994, 33)

The professional is not the only active and competent agent constructed
in the above example; nor is the professional constructed as acting on
local people. Instead, the professional is positioned as a subject who
creates a space for deliberation and dialogue between different groups.

In this discourse, local people are recognised as heterogeneous,
and importantly, the Coalition discourse avoids reifying local people
in terms of racial, ethnic, gender, sexual and ability differences. The
identities that are constructed between the professional and local people
are democratic and non-hierarchical and as a result, local people are
defined as active and competent subjects.

As I demonstrated with the Democracy and Empowerment
discourses, the binary distinction between professional/local people
in the Coalition discourse has been subverted and replaced with an
identity in which professionals and local people are indistinguishable.
This new identity construction is made possible by the discursive
practice of emphasising coalition building and turning private troubles
into public issues. Building alliances across difference means that the
work of the professional is not about using expertise to act on passive
groups but about facilitating dialogue between competent subjects in
order to take collective action and to address common problems shared
by all marginalised groups. This process of facilitating dialogue, building
non-hierarchical relationships and decentring unequal identities, I
argue, is due to the Coalition discourse's use of anti-racist feminist
ideas and social practices:

> [Feminist community development] aims to eliminate the
> dichotomies that are often created between the community
> and the power structure and between the organisers and the
> community...[Feminist community development] views
> the organiser as an equal with the community. Rather than
> be an expert at all facets of organising, the organiser both
> learns from and gives to the community. (Bradshaw, Soifer
> and Gutierrez 1994, 29–30)

Because the hierarchy of identities between professionals and local
people have been undermined, this creates the space and opportunity
for local people to be recognised and respected as active, competent
and effective subjects. More than any other competing ideology

in community development, anti-racist feminism seems to provide community development with the language and social practices to make real its claims about supporting equality and self-determination of marginalised groups.

## Conclusions

In this chapter I identified and analysed two key discourses and identity constructions of American community development in the 1990s. The micropolitics of community development of this moment are dominated by the capitulation to neoliberalism of the Democratic Party under Bill Clinton. This widespread acceptance of neoliberalism helps to shape community development at this time. The Revitalisation discourse constructs the goal of community development to build the resilience of poor communities to both withstand the vagaries and take advantage of the free market. By marketising communities, local people and private enterprises are able to build and exploit the social, political and economic assets of a given neighbourhood and in doing so capture a share of economic prosperity. In opposition to this, the Coalition discourse constructs the goal of community development to build a civil society in which the discrete differences of identity and issue-based groups are recognised and these groups are supported to build solidarity to struggle for equality and social justice for all marginalised groups.

It is important to emphasise how the presence or absence of participatory democracy and anti-racist feminism significantly affects the identity constructions in the Coalition and Revitalisation discourses. Where these ideas are present, identity constructions are more socially just and equal. By rejecting the hierarchical binaries between professionals and local people, community development discourses derived from participatory democratic and anti-racist feminist principles seek to construct local people as active and competent agents for social change. Where these ideas and practices are absent – as in the case of the majority of community development discourses I have analysed – identity constructions are derived from problematic binaries that construct professionals as active subjects and local people as passive and bewildered objects.

I will now turn to the final analysis chapter of this book and explore how the convergence of Left/Right politics and community development takes shape in the British context.

# CHAPTER SEVEN

# Privatising public life: neoliberalism and the dilemmas of British community development

## Introduction

In the last chapter, I analysed how the micropolitics of community development in America were deeply influenced by the popularity and dominance of neoliberalism. The official discourse of institutional actors did not seek to challenge the key tenets of neoliberalism and instead reconstructed community development as an instrument of the free market. For oppositional actors, community development was constructed as a way to counter neoliberalism and build coalitions across difference in order to support a vibrant civil society based on equality and social justice. This chapter focuses on the micropolitics of community development in Britain from 1992 to 1997 and I have identified two discourses for analysis. The 'Participation' discourse is constituted by the texts, language and practices of international and domestic institutions, such as the United Nations, the World Bank and the UK government, which seek to reconstruct community development as the means by which the poor become active and entrepreneurial citizens who participate in partnerships with the state and the market in order to tackle social problems. I shall argue that community development, as understood by the Participation discourse, should be seen primarily as a tool for the on-going neoliberal project of shrinking the welfare state and marketising social relationships. In contrast to this, the 'Transformation' discourse is constituted by the texts, language and practices of socialist, feminist and anti-racist community development practitioners and academics seeking to subvert the neoliberal colonialisation of community development. I shall argue that the Transformation discourse seeks to construct community development as a process of critical consciousness whereby community groups seek new forms of citizenship and radical democracy to resist the privatisation of the state and public spaces.

I will begin my analysis with a short contextual discussion of the formation and structure of the community development discourses during this politically salient moment. I will briefly discuss the legacy of the neoliberal project under Margaret Thatcher especially in terms of the redefinition of key concepts such as the welfare state, citizenship and the market. I will then turn to analyse the texts and identity constructions that constitute the Participation and Transformation discourses

## Thatcher's legacy in the 1990s

> The strength of Thatcherism is its ability to ventriloquise [sic] the genuine anxieties of working class experience. The declining economy and reduced living standards are explained by the expensive burden of public services... Frustrations with unresponsive and undemocratic welfare services are equated with the overweening bureaucracy of socialism. The ideology is...a full-throated affirmation of some simple dichotomies: welfare state, collectivism, socialism/freedom, liberty, choice. (Golding 1983, 10–11)

Although forced from office in 1990 after the disastrous introduction of the Poll Tax, Thatcher's legacy was already assured. The three-term Prime Minister presided over important transformations of the post-war welfare state, the promotion of monetarist economic policies and the reaffirmation of radical individualism in British politics (Gyford 1991; Cochrane 1993; Burns et al. 1994). While it is beyond the scope of this book to discuss the Thatcher project at length, this section will focus on the legacy of Thatcherism for our understandings of citizenship and the state provision of social welfare.

In terms of social welfare, Thatcherism can be understood as a commitment to radical individualism and the limited collective provision of social protection (Golding 1983, 9–12; Kingdom 1992, 44–56; Faulks 1998, 77–80). Thatcherism interprets individualism in terms of negative rights, maximum individual liberty and meritocracy[8]. Individual liberty is championed because freedom can only be achieved by self-sufficiency and self-reliance. Freedom cannot be handed down from or mediated by the state: 'The primary duty of individuals was to themselves: duty to others was not an act of citizenship, but of charity' (Faulks 1998, 85). Negative rights – the ability not to be interfered with in pursuing one's self-interest – is what counts in Thatcherism

---

[8]    Given the shared political philosophies of Thatcher and Reagan, it is no surprise that each advances similar interpretations of the welfare state and the free market.

because it is by relying on oneself (and one's family and kinship networks) that an individual is able to achieve self-determination. By only looking out for one's self, an individual is able to make free choices and meaningful decisions about the kind of life she wishes to lead. This focus on radical individualism is important as it rejects any notion of social solidarity, that individual citizens are connected to or responsible for each other. Thus being a good citizen is a limited proposition – it simply extends to respecting and preserving each citizen's liberty through non-interference. With this radical freedom comes true equality based on merit. Individuals, through hard work and entrepreneurship, should be able to climb the social ladder without any arbitrary support from the state or constraints imposed on them by gender, race or class. Thus in relation to social welfare and community development, Thatcher's legacy in the 1990s – as seen in the policy platforms of both the Conservative government under John Major and the Labour government under Tony Blair – is about redefining notions of fairness and equality.

Thatcherism constructs fairness and equality as being determined by the competition between free individuals rather than being controlled and sanctioned by the state:

> The ideal type of citizenship…is one in which the state serves the individual and protects their freedoms in civil society…All citizens have the right to freedom in a negative sense, but have no right to be helped by the state or other individuals to achieve an equal ability to exercise their freedom. In a sense citizens have rights to inequality…and to rise and fall in the market place which does not discriminate on moral or personal grounds. (Faulks 1998, 66–7)

Thatcherism's radical individualism necessitates a decoupling of the responsibility for the collective provision of welfare from the idea of a 'good citizen'. Because fairness and equality can only be ensured when individuals are unconstrained by fellow citizens and the state, the legitimacy of state-sponsored welfare is subverted. Thatcherism rejects the idea of the collective provision of welfare because it interprets the welfare state as promoting dependency and reducing an individual's ability to be self-sufficient. To support the self-determination and equality of individual citizens, the state should not intervene as a corrective to the competition between free individuals. The only institution that can support the radical individualism as envisioned by Thatcherism is the free market. It is in the free market where individuals are given the space and opportunity to innovate and compete in order to get ahead. 'It is impossible to underestimate the importance of the concept of the market in British politics; nowhere is the ideology of individualism more purely distilled' (Kingdom 1992, 57). Along with the redefinition of fairness and equality, we also see that the other legacy of Thatcherism is the substitution of the state for the market as the primary vehicle to ensure freedom, equality and prosperity.

In terms of policy priorities, we can see how both Major, from 1990 to 1997, and Blair, from 1997 to 2007, reconciled themselves to Thatcher's legacy. Using the language of the market in terms of contracting out public services and redefining citizens into consumers, Major and Blair continued Thatcher's revolution of shrinking and privatising the welfare state. This can be seen in Major's Citizen Charter and Blair's idea of active citizenship. For Major, contained within the Citizen Charter was the state's commitment to customer service, the promotion of individual choice and the state's accountability to individual consumers: 'The aim...was...to deliver to citizens, consumer rights as part of a wider commitment to market rights, which would provide assurance of the quality of the services provided through government spending' (Faulks 1998, 135). The focus of the Citizen Charter is not about strengthening social rights but providing citizens with the rights afforded to consumers in the marketplace. In doing so, at least in theory, the market helps to regulate freedom of choice and voice for consumers to demand better quality services from an array of social welfare providers. For Major, the goal was about transforming citizens into consumers because it is only the free market that is able to deliver authentic freedom and choice to citizens.

For Blair, we can see Thatcher's legacy in terms of his focus on active citizenship and the 'rights and responsibilities' agenda in social welfare provision. Through Labour's so-called 'Third Way' (similar to Clinton's New Democrat communitarian agenda in the US, which I discussed in Chapter Six) the innovations of the free market were to be combined with a commitment to social welfare to produce more efficient services and encourage individual self-reliance. This 'modernisation' of the state can be seen most clearly in Blair's model of welfare reform (which shares many features with Clinton's workfare agenda):

> The welfare system is a proud creation. But reform is essential if we are to realise our vision of a modern nation and a decent and fair society...We aim to break the cycle of dependency and insecurity and empower all citizens to lead a dignified and fulfilling life. We need a 'contract' between

citizens and the state with rights and responsibilities. (Department of Social Security 1998 quoted in Dwyer 2000, 7)

It is important to briefly note that oppositional politics were not absent during this moment. As I argued in Chapter Five, from the late 1970s onwards socialist politics were in crisis in the UK, as elsewhere, and this crisis was deepened by the collapse of the Soviet Bloc from 1989 onwards. The problems with socialism were so severe that Francis Fukuyama (1990) infamously predicted the 'end of history' with the triumph of free market capitalism and liberal democracy. Although the decline of socialism was mirrored with the strengthening of new social movements such as feminism, anti-racism, gay rights and environmentalism, these disparate and fractured movements did not prove to be an effective counterbalance to the popularity of Thatcherism. Thus, as I argued in Chapter Five, this moment should be seen as a time of continued reorientation and reorganisation for left-wing politics in Britain.

In terms of the micropolitics of community development during this moment in time, we can see how the two discourses are formed and structured in response to these events. The Participation discourse is constituted by the language and practices of institutional actors advancing neoliberalism. As the British (and American) welfare states underwent a process of privatisation, other institutions such as the United Nations and the World Bank were also advancing neoliberal policies. We can see this process of the liberalisation of markets and privatisation of state services most clearly in Britain with the contracting out of public services and the creation of a mixed economy for social welfare; in the World Bank's structural adjustment policies; and the UN's focus on 'people-friendly markets' (Faulks 1998; Taylor et al. 2000). These domestic and international institutional actors were seeking to harness the innovation of the market in order to support the self-determination and liberty of individuals. For these actors, community development is defined as a process by which consumer-citizens learn self-reliance and entrepreneurial skills by participating in the free market. In addition, the Participation discourse is also formed by reconceptualising ideas of social citizenship. Since the decentralisation and privatisation of welfare services and decision-making is a key goal of neoliberalism, in this discourse I identify a renewed focus on consumer-citizen's 'participation' in service planning and delivery whereby the burden of social protection is transferred from the state to individuals and community groups.

The Participation discourse is constituted by the language and social practices of official actors in British central and local government and in international institutions such as the United Nations and the World Bank. I have included a number of texts from international institutions as partly constituting the Participation discourse for a variety of reasons. First, the British community development texts make direct references to the work of the World Bank and the UN as models of practice to be replicated (as in the Participation discourse) or to be opposed (as in the Transformation discourse). Second, this internationalisation of debate demonstrates the totalising aspects of neoliberalism that both the Participation and Transformation discourses interpellate in order to support their ideas and practices (Gyford 1991; Gerson 1993; Burns et al. 1994; Lal 1994; UNDP 1993; Barr 1991; Faulks 1998; Taylor et al. 2000).

For the Transformation discourse, the dominance of neoliberalism is also a constitutive element. Informed by neo-Marxist, feminist and anti-racist actors, this discourse is about re-legitimising socialism as an effective opposition to neoliberalism, by tempering it with notions of radical democracy and, to a lesser extent, the analyses of various new social movements (Jacobs and Popple 1994; Waddington 1994; Popple 1995; Taylor 1995; Collins and Lister 1996; Meagher and Tett 1996; Mayo 1997; Miller and Ahmad 1997; Shaw and Martin 2000). By emphasising collective forms of social citizenship, these actors argue that meaningful individual freedom and participation can only be achieved when citizens build solidarity by ensuring the social protection of others. For the Transformation discourse, community development is the process by which local people learn the duties and obligations of citizenship in terms of struggling to democratise the state and building solidarity for collective social protection. Community development is also the way in which citizens resist and subvert neoliberal practices that seek to reduce the state and privatise public life.

I will now move on to analyse the Participation and Transformation discourses and identities in further detail.

## The Participation discourse: privatising public life

The Participation discourse is constituted by the texts, language and practices of official actors in international and domestic institutions seeking to reconstruct social citizenship and the relationship between the state, the market and citizens. In the Participation discourse, community development is constructed as a tool to redefine social relationships in order to reconcile citizens to the new order of a marketised and privatised public life. Through the promotion of public and private sector partnerships and the participation of local people within these structures, the Participation discourse seeks to deliver local people to these new privatised spaces in order for people to learn self-reliance, entrepreneurship and independence from the state. For instance, here is the United Nation Development Programme (UNDP 1993, 4–5) discussing the need to combine the market and state:

> People should guide both the state and the market, which need to work in tandem, with people sufficiently empowered to exert a more effective influence over both... Changing markets to make them more people-friendly would start by maintaining the dynamism of markets but adding other measures that allow many more people to capitalise on the advantages that markets offer.

The Participation discourse undertakes a series of interrelated practices in order to reconstruct the role of community development. Specifically, it sets up a binary of market/state in order to highlight the inefficiencies of the state and the superiority of the market; it reconstructs social citizenship away from positive social rights to negative consumer rights which correspond to the dynamism of the market; and finally it constructs private–public partnerships and participation structures as a way for newly constructed 'consumer-citizens' to benefit from marketised principles and practices (UNDP 1993, 4–5; Barr 1991, 134–48; Faulks 1998, 132–7; Taylor et al. 2000, 29–30).

The discourse first constructs a binary of market/state in order to demonstrate the superiority of the market in delivering innovation, efficiency and effectiveness in social welfare. The state is constructed as both old-fashioned and self-serving. In this new era of globalisation, the state is no longer able to competently deal with issues of social welfare on its own – the state needs the market for support and guidance. As the United Nations Development Programme (UNDP 1993, 4–5) argues:

> Now that so many countries have embarked on strategies of economic liberalisation and privatisation...new partnerships are needed between the state and the market... to accommodate the rise of people's aspirations and the steady decline of the nation-state...The nation-state is now too small for the big things and too big for the small.

The state also needs the market to bring efficiency and innovation to paternalistic bureaucrats who promote the public's dependency on inefficient services as a way to justify their position:

> Too often, public sector organisations seem to deliver services that were designed to suit the providers rather than the recipients....There must no longer be a hiding place for sloppy standards, lame excuses and attitudes that patronise the public. (Home Office 1995, 7)

In order to overcome these problems of the state, the Participation discourse focuses on the primacy of the market and its values of individual choice, competition and efficiency to transform social welfare services:

> Individuals should be able to express preference and make decisions about the services they receive from the state or in the market place. The greater the choice, the better the services...By making public services more like private industries, services would be rendered more effective and efficient. (Faulks 1998, 133)

By constructing the state as inefficient and then by establishing the primacy of the market in delivering choice and efficiency for the public, the Participation discourse is able to reconstruct notions of social citizenship. Citizenship is effectively privatised in this discourse. Through the prism of the market, the public are transformed into consumers invested with marketised rights and expectations of choice, competition and quality: 'The consumer making judgements on price and quality in the shopping centre would be the contemporary symbol of economic democracy' (Gyford 1991, 18). As the state-sponsored Community Development Foundation argues, consumerism leads to efficiency, empowerment and better democracy:

> The emphasis on choice and user-run services...has been an important element in community empowerment. The continued interest in user involvement in public services along with the expansion of consumer or citizens' charters has gone some way towards redressing the balance between providers and their 'clients'. Increasingly, professional service provision is seen to include responsiveness to user demand and need. (Taylor et al. 2000, 29–30)

In the Participation discourse, however, consumer-citizens should not be interpreted as passive recipients of services. By expanding the opportunities for consumer choice through the mixed economy of welfare and by exercising the right of voice and exit in underperforming services, consumer-citizens can articulate their dissatisfaction and vote with their feet if the state fails to meet expectations. Thus an important part of privatised citizenship in the Participation discourse is constructing consumers as willing and able to take on the burden of service provision in order to ensure services meet local needs:

> Communities should analyse what is produced and consumed by local people and then seek to meet these needs more locally. Communities should produce for themselves what it is possible and reasonable for them to produce... If one looked at all the goods and services in a local area and tried to replace them with a community-owned or delivered systems, the amount that could be shifted to local control would be a surprisingly high percentage. (Taylor et al. 2000, 36)

Once again, we can see the state being further marginalised as privatised consumer-citizens infused with an entrepreneurial spirit learn from the marketplace take on the role of service provider for social welfare. For the Participation discourse, the highest expression of civic virtue is individual responsibility and entrepreneurship. The link between the citizen and the state has been replaced with that of the consumer and the market and any sense of social solidarity has been subverted. In this context of a marketised state and a privatised citizen, the Participation discourse redefines the role for community development.

Unlike previous moments in my analysis of the discursive history of British community development, under neoliberalism and at this moment in time, community development as a discourse and as a set of discrete social practices is utterly transformed. Rather than community development being focused on the redistribution of wealth and power to the working class, as in the Structuralist discourse in Chapter Three, or even the more modest and quantifiable objectives of connecting people better to the local state as in the post-Marxist and Realist discourses of Chapter Five, community development as understood in the Participation discourse is constructed as a process to deliver the public to various neoliberal policy processes. Through participation in public-private partnerships, community development supports the inculcation of people into marketised values of citizenship. Here are two examples of this process:

> By facilitating participation, community development supports policies for decent services and public participation in decision-making. Under compulsory competitive tendering, it has a new role in supporting community-based organisations to tender for contracts, bringing services and jobs to areas of high unemployment. (Blackman 1994, 142)

> The task for community development must be to develop new forms of production of goods, information and services, which release the potential and resources of all parts of the community...This will involve new partners in new forms of management and ownership, which provide genuine choice and whose logic flows from the user rather than the administrative demands of the provider. Often there will be scope for users to become producers. (Taylor et al. 2000, 35–6)

As the above quotes demonstrate, community development is to be used as a tool for transferring the responsibility for social welfare to these newly created citizen-consumers. Controlling service provision is constructed as an empowering act in which citizen-consumers take an active and leading role.

In an important hegemonic practice, the Participation discourse redefines the meanings of 'partnership' and 'participation'. Rather than partnership denoting a cooperative relationship between citizens and participation meaning democratic encounters in a polis, partnership and participation are reconstructed as central features of neoliberal community development. Partnerships are marketised spaces whereby the state and citizen-consumers learn innovative practices from the private sector in order to tackle social problems. In the context of a weak state and privatised citizens, it is the process of learning from the market in terms of choice, competition and efficiency that community development is positioned:

> The possibilities exist for creative partnerships involving statutory, voluntary, private and community sectors in building a raft of...provision within a locality. Where community experience and expertise is limited, such partnerships...may be used to foster and support the

emergence of healthy enterprises and minimise risks. (Barr 1991, 145)

Citizen-consumers' participation within partnerships is not so much about democracy but about building in efficiencies to service provision. It is important to note that participation is understood as a very time-limited and constrained activity that is tied to the particular partnership or service provided:

> Participation is a process by which people – especially disadvantaged people – can exercise influence over policy formation, design alternatives, investment choices, management and monitoring of development interventions in their communities...Participation is not a discrete event that may occur only at specific point in a project's history but instead may be realised over the entire lifecycle of a development project. (Gerson 1993, 5)

In this sense, participation is not a 'public good' in itself. Rather, participation is important because it allows citizen-consumers to express needs and this allows for the more efficient planning and delivery of services:

> Whilst democracy promotes liberty, it may not promote opulence, which depends upon an efficient market economy and which in turn does not require a democratic form of government for its maintenance....Mass participation through pressure in a democracy may harm rather than aid the attainment of both the ends of opulence and liberty... Thus [participation]...must depend upon the actual merits of each case, namely whether this provides the least cost mode of provision. (Lal 1994, 6)

Despite the Participation discourse's reconstruction of the nature and function of community development, my analysis of identity constructions demonstrates identity constructions consistent with other moments in time I have previously analysed.

The Participation discourse constructs a two-pronged identity of modernisers who are composed of both policy makers and conservative community development practitioners. What these two distinct groups have in common is framing the socio-economic transformation of Britain since the late 1970s as an opportunity rather than a threat for citizen-consumers. The modernisers see the privatisation of the state and the infusion of marketised values in the state as a way of opening up previously unaccountable institutions to outside influence. The neoliberal practices of decentralisation of service provision, compulsory competitive tendering and the mixed economy for welfare are all ways to break down the bureaucratic paternalism of the state, make the state more responsive to local needs and to maximise individual freedom, choice and aspirations. Here is an interesting construction of the modernisers seeking to position themselves as the real democrats in the neoliberal transformations of the state:

> Placing people at the centre of political and economic change...calls for nothing less than revolution in our thinking...Every institution – and every policy action – should be judged by one critical test – how does it meet the genuine aspirations of the people? (UNDP 1993, 8)

The construction of the modernisers is also based on notions of anti-elitism and populism. Because one of the tenets of neoliberalism is the maximum possible freedom for the individual, modernisers are constructed as champions of individual liberty and choice and defenders of these freedoms from the tyranny of the abstractions of the state and of society:

> Individual liberty is the foundation – the most important value to be protected...It is dangerous to put the needs of society...above those of any individual...The concept of society... reifies something which cannot have an identity or will outside of or separate from the individuals that make it up (Faulks 1998, 55)

Two marginalised identities are also constructed in this discourse: state bureaucrats and local people. As I have previously discussed, state bureaucrats are constructed as paternalistic and self-serving, their only interest being to maintain their own power and influence within various public sector institutions. It is only through the introduction of market principles – in terms of consumer choice, customer service and accountability – that this particular actor can be co-opted and transformed.

In terms of local people, as I have demonstrated in previous chapters, the public are constructed along contradictory lines. On the one hand, local people are defined as passive objects in the Participation discourse.

Despite the radical individualism of the discourse, local people are often constructed as objects of policy and intervention rather than as subjects invested with agency. The assumption underlying the construction of individuals as consumers is that they are currently passive and dependent objects of the paternalistic welfare state:

> Following the Second World War, citizens became increasingly dependent upon the state to solve their problems, and this dependency rendered citizens impotent in the performance of their responsibilities (Faulks 1998, 127)

Thus local people need to be transformed, their capacity built, through a process of community development, into self-reliant, independent citizen-consumers who have been weaned off the nanny state. Thus, rather paradoxically, local people are also constructed as latent entrepreneurs who need community development interventions in order to transform themselves from dependent objects of the state to active neoliberal subjects:

> Community development helps to create a pool of skilled and interested local people who can become involved in public life at all levels: managing a school or a housing estate; working with government agencies to plan more sensitive services; or providing information, advice and advocacy to help services users choose the provision they need (Taylor et al. 2000, 26)

Once again, I think there is a problem here with the way the idea of agency is operationalised in the discourse. For local people, agency is something to be mediated and handed down by professionals. Policy makers and community development professionals are always constructed as possessing agency and having the power to distribute it among various individuals and groups. The public are often defined as lacking agency and thus requiring the actions of professionals to transform them into competent subjects. As I have demonstrated in previous chapters, this understanding of agency inadvertently sets up hierarchical relationships between professionals and local people and this hierarchy appears to undermine the Participation discourse's claims of promoting individual liberty.

I will now turn to analyse the Transformation discourse.

## The Transformation discourse: reclaiming radical community development?

The Transformation discourse is constituted by the texts, language and practices of socialist, feminist and anti-racist community development practitioners and theorists seeking to subvert the dominant neoliberal approaches to community development, citizenship and the state. I have chosen 'Transformation' to describe this discourse because it signals a change in the language of radicalism within British community development. Rather than community development focusing on revolution or the redistribution of wealth, it is constructed as a way in which local people develop 'critical consciousness' in order to resist neoliberal practices and transform the practice of democracy in Britain:

> The real challenge, and in sharp contrast to the current emphasis on consumer feedback, is the extent to which [community development] can play a role in the repoliticisation of public life within civil society. There is a growing need for the creation of public fora at local, city and regional levels where the focus is on both the politics of everyday life and the management and organisation of the social world. (Miller and Ahmad 1997, 280)

Three key concepts are central to Transformation discourse: citizenship, participation and public space; I will discuss each of these in turn. First, rather than citizenship being defined as consumerism and individualism as we have seen the in the Participation discourse, the Transformation discourse focuses on re-establishing the relationship between citizenship, social welfare and collectivism. The discourse advances an expansive idea of citizenship: the focus is on promoting the civil, political and social rights and duties of an individual in a democratic polis. Citizenship is the combination of participation and decision-making about the common good, the collective right to social welfare and the duty to ensure the collective provision of social protection. According to the Transformation discourse, this proactive, positive and collective construction of citizenship is the only way to ensure that people are able to practice their rights and duties in a democracy:

> Education for citizenship means...the nurturing of a capacity and willingness to question, to probe...to see through obfuscation and lies...The cultivation of an awareness that

the quest for individual fulfilment needs to be combined with the larger demands of solidarity and concern for the public good. (Miliband 1994, 34)

This focus on citizenship as the practice and fulfilment of rights links to the next key concept of the Transformation discourse. Participation is the practice of citizenship in public spaces. Alluding to ancient Athens, participation is constructed as citizen engagement in the agora. Thus in opposition to the idea of participation as tied to a particular neoliberal development project as seen the Participation discourse, the Transformation discourse's antagonistic construction of participation is a much broader conceit. Here are Shaw and Martin (2000, 409) outlining their view of participation:

> The politics of the state now needs to be reconstructed in ways which strengthen civil society and political life both outside and inside the state...The democratic state needs civil society...it is in civil society that people learn to be the active citizens they become in the democratic state... Consequently, it is in the relationship between civil society and the state that the process of reconstructing citizenship and democracy must begin.

Participation is a two-pronged process by which people learn to become citizens and it is also the way in which the state is democratised. Because the Transformation discourse is about opposing the privatisation of citizenship and the state, it seeks to redefine citizenship and the practices of citizens in order to democratise the relationships and spaces between citizens, the state and the market. Here is Taylor (1995, 107) discussing this point:

> People's lives have been privatised. Many things which used to be done collectively can or have to be done individually...There seems less need for any kind of public or even collective involvement...Ways must be found to engage people and convince them that there is a point in making a commitment to a public sphere which they feel has failed them or is simply seen as irrelevant in a consumerist age.

The normative value that the Transformation discourse attaches to participation is directly linked to the discourse's emphasis on public space. By opposing the privatisation of the state and citizenship, the discourse constructs public space as the site of democratic social relations between citizens and between citizens and the state. Public space is the sphere is which citizens encounter each other and make decisions about the common good:

> The very notion of citizenship implies the polis, the city, the community, the collective realm, where the performance of obligations, both 'private' and 'public' derives from participation in a political community. It is a two-way relationship and the concept of citizenship has an inextricable connection with the notion of democracy. (Waddington 1994, 10)

With participation and public space constructed in relation to the practice of democracy, public–private partnerships (which I discussed in relation to the Participation discourse) are a deeply problematic concept within the Transformation discourse. On the one hand, partnerships are constructed as potentially influential and democratic spaces whereby local people are able to participate in decisions that affect their lives: 'There are examples of partnerships which have been…part of strategies to tackle paternalism, to empower service users and carers and to reinforce and develop collective approaches to social solidarity and reciprocity' (Mayo 1997, 8). On the other hand, partnerships can be mechanisms to deliver citizens to neoliberal policy agendas: 'Participation and partnership were simple euphemisms used to mask the unpleasant realities involved in securing the compliance of community organisations with an externally-imposed agenda' (Collins and Lister 1996, 38).

Because the language and practices of community development are being colonised by the neoliberal Participation discourse, the Transformation discourse seeks to position community development in such a way as to effectively subvert both the linguistic and practice-based co-optation of community development. In ways similar to the 1968 Structural discourse I discussed in Chapter Three, the Transformation discourse constructs community development as a process of democratisation in which citizens develop critical consciousness to oppose the hegemonic practices of the marketised state. Here are two examples of this construction of critical consciousness:

> Community workers should not be afraid of looking at ways in which to introduce alternative views and political ideas to

the community work process…The development of critical consciousness together with opportunities for activists to synthesise their experiences should be crucial elements in a contemporary radical practice. (Cooke 1996, 21)

[Community workers should] help people reflect on the contradictions between their everyday lived experience of oppression and the prevailing ideology rather than just accepting the world as it is…This process of praxis based on critical reflection and action enables the community worker…to develop critical dialogue [with groups] which challenge pessimistic and fatalistic thinking about how the world works. (Meagher and Tett 1996, 129)

'Critical consciousness', 'critical dialogue' and 'critical reflection' are important patterns in the language of the Transformation discourse. The discourse appears to be interpellating the earlier Structuralist discourse and its practices of combating false consciousness and developing organic intellectuals. The Transformation discourse does not use the term 'false consciousness', but because the discourse does construct community development as a way to foster the critical consciousness of citizens – the need for people to look beyond common sense understandings of the world and understand how they are being co-opted into the undemocratic processes of neoliberalism – I think this amounts to the same practices. Indeed it is during this moment in time that Freire (1970) and Gramsci (1984) re-enter the language of community development and their ideas are incorporated into the Transformation discourse. Here are two examples:

Gramsci provides us with an understanding of the key concepts of hegemony, ideology and the role of intellectuals, while Freire has developed the notion of 'conscientization' and the use of particular educational methods to help people to perceive, interpret, criticise and finally transform the world around them. (Jacobs and Popple 1994, 25)

Freire's view is that in struggling to change their world people also change their understanding of their world. In turn this changes the types of change which they seek and the ways in which they seek it. (Collins and Lister 1996, 32)

As the above quotes demonstrate, the Transformation discourse seeks to position community development as a linguistic and psychological process in which citizens are 'decolonised' in their thinking and actions through critiques of the 'dominant ideology'.

I will now turn to analyse identity constructions in the Transformation discourse. This discourse constructs an almost mirror image of the professional Gramscian organic intellectual that I identified in the Structuralist discourse in Chapter Three. While this Gramscian professional in the Transformation discourse is not constructed to foment revolution, this radical professional is constructed as an educator and facilitator of critical dialogue and action among community groups in order to counter and subvert neoliberalism. Here are two examples of the professional as a facilitator of dialogue and action:

> Progressive community work is a liberating force that recognises the inherent contradictions in capitalism while providing a practice that centres on developing a critical dialogue and increasing political consciousness... Community work...is engaged in liberating the minds and encouraging and supporting the actions of the disadvantaged. (Jacobs and Popple 1994, 33–4)

> If the development of a political analysis amongst those with whom we work is still the principal aim of radical community work...[this] can only be achieved by the introduction of systematic reflection and more structured educational opportunities within the community work process. (Cooke 1996, 20)

Despite the construction of professionals as facilitators of critical consciousness – the discourse is fractured in its constructions of local people. In some texts, the discourse continues the pattern of hierarchical identities between professional/local people; while in other texts, we are starting to see the breakdown of this binary. Here are two indicative examples of the contradictory construction of local people:

> In a globalising economy it is not uncommon to feel powerless to influence or respond to key decisions that fundamentally effect [sic] our current and future lives... Consequently there is no doubt in our minds that there is much that needs to be done to enable people to regain or

experience some sense of self-confidence and self-worth. (Miller and Ahmad 1997, 277–8)

New forms of service provision and production are required which not only release resources…but also change the power relationship between producer and user, recognising that service users are producers of their own welfare and not passive recipients. (Taylor 1995, 109)

From the first quote we can see how citizens are constructed as passive and powerless and need community development to order to provide them with agency. In the second quote, the public are constructed as competent and active subjects in relation to the state and social welfare professionals.

In addition to the above contradictory constructions, local people are no longer constructed as homogeneous – issues of race, gender, disability and sexuality now influence the Transformation discourse's construction of citizens. For example:

Instead of having a unitary view of the working class which is based on an outdated view of white, male, workers engaged in heavy, manual work, the emphasis needs to be on the way in which class position is mediated by geographical location, sexuality, age, race and gender. (Meagher and Tett 1996, 131)

This is an important change in the structure of a community development discourse in the British context. Finally, the public are constructed as raced, classed and gendered and difference is beginning to be recognised in the British community development tradition.

## Conclusions

This chapter has focused on the micropolitics of community development during the 1992 to 1997 politically salient moment in Britain. I first discussed Thatcher's legacy and demonstrated how her views on citizenship, the state and the market exerted a powerful influence on the politics and policy priorities of both the Major and Blair governments. I then moved on to discuss how neoliberal hegemony influenced the formation and structure of the community development discourses during this moment in time. As I have demonstrated, British community development ideas and practices were being co-opted by neoliberalism and it was being deployed as a way to undermine the welfare state, promote individualism and privatise public life. The Participation discourse constructs community development as a process by which to deliver consumer-citizens to state policy processes in order to inculcate them with the values and practices of the free market. In doing so, consumer-citizens learn self-reliance, self-determination and experience radical liberty in order to make free choices about their lives. In opposition to this, the Transformation discourse constructs community development as the process of critical education in order to build and sustain radical citizenship and social solidarity.

The Participation and Transformation discourses continue the pattern of constructing questionable identity constructions for local people. In the British context in particular, the way in which agency is operationalised, in terms of it being controlled and mediated by professionals in order to benefit local people, reinforces rather than breaks down hierarchical identity constructions between professionals and local people. During this moment, however, we also see the emergence of different ways of representing local people. For the Transformation discourse, local people are also constructed as active agents and are recognised as heterogeneous in terms of race, class, gender, disability and sexuality. This is an important expansion in the category of local people especially because in the British context, the discourses, up to this moment, have not effectively recognised difference or constructed local people as possessing agency. This transformation in the construction of local people echoes the developments I have charted in the American context especially in relation to the democratic identity constructions constituted by anti-racist feminisms.

# CHAPTER EIGHT

# Between economic crisis and austerity: what next for community development in America and Britain?

The aim of this book was to examine the contentious micropolitics of American and British community development since 1968. By analysing community development discourses in two countries and across three politically salient historical moments, I have attempted to demonstrate how the ideas, discourses, practices and identities that reproduce inequality and disrespect have become dominant within community development and have, at times, systematically marginalised competing approaches that seek to construct egalitarian and democratic identities and social practices in this field. Using a post-structuralist discourse analysis methodology helped me approach fairly well known data – the community development texts – in a new way. Focusing on identity constructions is a powerful way of considering the claims and assumptions of community development and as a consequence, I was able to problematise the basic assumptions that give impetus to the theory and practice of community development in both countries.

The analysis that I offer in this book has repeatedly problematised the grand narrative of community development. Rather than community development in either country being a transformative process of progressive social change, frequently it is a process of policy makers and professionals subjecting local people to patronising, disrespectful and undemocratic ideas, language and practices. In particular, community development appears to be predicated on a range of problematic identity constructions. More often than not, the professional, the radical or the policy maker in the dominant community development discourses in America and Britain are always invested with agency while local people are constructed as a passive, bewildered and incorrigible object to be acted on by the professional. The reason why these identity constructions dominate community development theory and practice seems to hinge on the particular way in which agency is operationalised by the majority of community development discourses.

Agency is objectified by most of the discourses. What I mean is that agency is understood as a possession that can be given or taken away from individuals and groups. Using the idea of agency in this way means that different types of people can be easily categorised as possessing or lacking the ability to control their lives. As a result, community development is defined as the process of professionals mediating, regulating and controlling other people's development of agency. This approach can of course be justified in a number of different ways in terms of confidence building, developing leadership skills and building the capacity for collective action. The problem I find with this approach is that it is based on questionable normative assumptions about the different subject positions professionals and local people occupy. In the majority of the discourses I analysed, professionals always possess agency while local people always lack agency. The discourses give various reasons why local people lack agency: it may be rooted in structural discrimination or it could be the result of pathological individual failings. That professionals appear to inherently possess the ability to act is never questioned in the discourses and this is very troubling for a field of practice that proclaims its fundamental orientation to social justice.

By using the idea of agency in this way, the discourses unintentionally create a democratic deficit in the community development process. By defining local people as deficient – for whatever political justification – creates a hierarchical and unequal relationship between local people and professionals. The result is that local people can never truly have power, be in control or determine their fates unless they first surrender themselves to outside intervention. For the majority of discourses to justify and legitimise their praxes and status, local people must be problematised in this way and professionals must take a lead role in the community development process.

That this unequal relationship between professionals and local people exists and persists over a 40-year period in both America and Britain and that this relationship is evident in various competing discourses that span left-wing and right-wing political thought is very troubling. The persistence of these problematic relations in community development appears to undermine the main assumptions and founding myths on which community development is based. According to my analysis, the majority of community development discourses do not seem to be able to support and facilitate the agency of local people; nor do they seem able to construct local people based on respect and equality in relation to professionals and policy makers. Community development, in many ways, can be seen as an oppressive social practice of imposing undemocratic and disrespectful identities and relationships onto local people – in the name of the self-determination of these very people.

Throughout this book I also demonstrated that the only community development discourses that appear to construct local people as active agents and authors of their lives, that attempt to facilitate the agency of local people and that aim to break down the hierarchical relations between professionals and local people are those that are constituted by the principles and practices of participatory democracy and anti-racist feminisms which I discussed in Chapters Two, Four, Six and Seven.

The assumption underpinning the Democracy discourse, which I analysed in Chapter Two, is that local people have the knowledge, skills and capacity to deliberate and take action on issues that are important to them. In this discourse, it is not that local people lack agency and thus need to be 'developed' or their 'capacity built' by organisers; it is that organisers need to create spaces for the democratic deliberations of local people and help facilitate the actions of local leadership. It is in the Democracy discourse where the promise of community development seems to be realised in two important ways. First, the Democracy discourse and its social practices seem to solve the vexed problem within community development about the balance between process and outcome in grassroots work. The discourse structures both process and outcome as equally important – the path a group takes to reach its goal is of equal importance as the goal itself. This way of representing the dual nature of community development is crucial because it sets up important identity constructions between organisers and local people. Second, because both process and outcome are important, this means that community development is constituted as a process of creating democratic spaces for debate and deliberation which is in turn a learning process for becoming a leader. An organiser does not act on objectified local people in this discourse. Rather, the process of community development seeks to displace the hierarchical relations between the community organiser and local people – and instead focus on the solidarity work and material struggles of building a democratic civil society in which all citizens are constituted as leaders and who have the ability organise and mobilise on issues that are important to them.

In the Empowerment, Coalition and (to a much more limited extent) Transformation discourses of the 1980s and 1990s that I discussed in Chapters Four, Six and Seven, we see the same discursive patterns at play. These three discourses focus on the defence and expansion of democratic spaces for the deliberation, participation and activism of the most marginalised. What the Democracy, Empowerment, Coalition and Transformation discourses share is a focus on the need for the democratisation of public spaces. The assumption driving each of these discourses is the understanding that equal access to public space and equality in public participation about the common good are crucial for a well functioning democracy. Thus, for these four discourses, it is the quality of democratic spaces in American and British public life – and not the agency and capacity of local people – that is problematised.

Given this analysis, it seems to me that the task for community development is to reconstruct its language and social practices in order to take democracy seriously. Rethinking the idea and practices of democracy can be an important way in which community development theorists, activists and professionals can approach these uncertain times. The 2008 global economic crisis and subsequent government austerity measures in Europe and America present an important challenge to the meaning and purpose of community development in America and Britain. The on-going crisis and austerity are dramatically reshaping the ways in which the public thinks about social justice, social welfare and the role of the state as a key arbiter of equality and rights.

Britain is currently undertaking a radical experiment in austerity that represents an unprecedented dismantling of the state (Taylor-Gooby 2011; Yeates et al. 2011). Dramatic spending reductions to key social welfare service budgets such as legal aid, unemployment benefits and social care mean that essential services are being reduced, eliminated or privatised with any willing provider from the private or third sectors contracted to replace the state (Bassel and Emejulu 2014). In the United States, 'austerity' is not named as such, but America's already meagre social safety net is also being pared back. Through sequestration, automatic and across the board spending cuts to the federal budget are being implemented in health, housing and education. Furthermore, because many aspects of social welfare are funded at the state and municipal levels, the capture of state legislatures by populist small government conservatives has meant that social welfare funding – particularly for public education and welfare – has been eliminated, reduced or privatised (Peck 2012; Davidson and Ward 2013).

With the state withdrawing from various parts of public life and with the idea of comprehensive social welfare for all being widely questioned by both policy makers and the public, what role might community development play in these uncertain times? In community development terms, current austerity measures are not a particularly 'new' challenge. As I have charted in this book, the dissolution of the post-war Keynesian welfare settlements and the rise of neoliberalism has had a profound impact on theory and practice of community development since the mid-1970s. Thus the challenge that the economic crisis and austerity poses is not necessarily the restructuring of the state or the rebalancing of relations between the state, the market and civil society, but the *comprehensiveness* of the state's withdrawal from public life, the deepening of precarity for already marginalised groups and the expansion of economic and social insecurity to new, previously privileged, social groups (Strolovitch 2013; Mayer 2013; Bassel and Emejulu 2014). In my view, it is community development's vital and immediate role to offer alternative and critical analyses and practices about the state, civil society organisations and political education in order to defend social justice, social welfare and social citizenship.

First, community development on both sides of the Atlantic must mount a meaningful defence of the state. The state can be a cumbersome, bureaucratic and self-serving institution that undermines individual liberty. It can also be a key guarantor and protector of equality and rights which makes individual liberty possible and meaningful. For community development, the state is both these things simultaneously. The state can undermine or suppress deliberative dialogue about the common good through 'invited spaces' that direct and control both the process and the outcomes of citizen debate. The state, however, can also support the democratic participation of the most marginalised through a system of social protection and welfare. Regardless of how the state in advanced capitalist countries is seen or experienced, it is important to bear in mind that it is not a monolith of either control or protection. Not engaging more directly and clearly with analyses and actions in relation to the state does not, of course, mean that the state 'withers away' from the politics of community development – the state is simply captured and directed by other more canny interest groups. By ceding ground on the state, those interested in community development and social justice may well be gifting the levers of state power to those most hostile to its potential for advancing equality and social justice. Reclaiming the state will be a problematic process for many supporters of community development, but it must be done in order to take democracy seriously.

Second, community development should resist the 'logic of entrepreneurship' that disciplines the actions of many grassroots-based organisations (Bassel and Emejulu 2014). The hegemony of neoliberalism means that, for many community development organisations to attract and keep funding, they are forced to mimic the ethos and behaviours of private sector organisations – they must reshape themselves to be and to be seen to be 'entrepreneurial', 'flexible' and 'innovative' (Bassel and Emejulu 2014). Indeed, as Choudry and Shragge argue (2011, 504–5):

> Community organisations have often shifted from organising active participants in social struggle to creating services for 'clients'…There is a movement in two

directions: community organisations act from the bottom-up, initiating services and programmes, while governments view 'community as policy', organising intervention and funding programmes that shape local activity to become responsible for a variety of services and programmes. This vertical relation has resulted in an increasingly collaborative relationship between community and government with diminished conflict.

This kind of organisational restructuring and rebalancing of relations between the state and civil society groups has real material consequences for organisations such as increased competition between community development agencies for funding and the commodification and marketisation of community development 'products and services'. As a result, solidarity within and between community development organisations is increasingly under threat and the ability for organisations to build coalitions to oppose austerity may be fatally weakened (for a detailed discussion of this see: Emejulu and Bassel 2013). My advocating for the abandonment of entrepreneurship as a model for community development practice presents a real dilemma for organizations, however. To survive, thrive and attempt to effect positive change for groups and neighbourhoods, community development organisations must attract sustainable funding. Being an 'entrepreneurial actor' is often the price that must be paid to ensure the future of the organisation. The question is whether this kind of entrepreneurial ethos is, in the long run, the best way to defend and expand the social citizenship rights of marginalised groups. For community development to take democracy seriously, I question the ability to fight the roll back of social welfare and social citizenship rights on the terms that neoliberalism sets.

Finally, for community development to take democracy seriously, it must re-engage with political education. While community organising, supporting local leaders and undertaking neighbourhood revitalisation efforts are important, all actors involved in a given community development process must have a vision for what drives these actions. Using the language of 'project completion', 'deliverables' and 'outputs' only reinforces the neoliberal colonialisation of community development organisations and projects. Critically analysing the politics and political economy of community development efforts can help individuals and groups consider what ideas and values are embedded in the actions they are undertaking and in whose interests these actions serve. Political education, though deeply unfashionable at this moment in time, is, in my view, the central purpose and driving force of community development. Bringing individuals together to think critically about themselves and the society in which they live, to think about social problems as both 'private troubles' and 'public issues' and to strategise and mobilise to take collective action are all part of the process of taking democracy seriously. Community development is a *political project*. In order to help counter neoliberalism and its disastrous consequences for marginalised communities, we must recognise, rather than ignore, the micropolitics of community development.

# References

Ackelsberg, M, 1988, 'Communities, resistance, and women's activism: Some implications for a democratic policy', in A Bookman, S Morgen, (eds) *Women and the Politics of Empowerment*, Philadelphia, PA: Temple University Press

Alinsky, SD, 1989 [1946], *Reveille for radicals*, New York, NY: Vintage

Alinsky, SD, 1971, *Rules for radicals: A pragmatic primer for realistic radicals*, New York, NY: Vintage

Althusser, L, 1970, 'Ideology and ideological state apparatuses', in L Althusser, *Lenin and philosophy and other essays*, London: New Left Books

Amin, A (ed), 1994, *Post-Fordism: A reader*, Oxford: Blackwell

Anderson, E, 1999, 'What is the point of equality?' *Ethics*, 109(2): 287–337

Baine, S, 1974, 'The political community', in D Jones, M Mayo, (eds) *Community Work One*, London: Routledge

Bagilhole, B, 2009, *Understanding equal opportunities and diversity: The social differentations and intersections of inequality*, Bristol: Policy Press

Baker, E, 1960, 'Bigger than a hamburger', in *The Southern patriot*, www.crmvet.org/docs/sncc2.htm

Baker, E, 1972, 'Developing community leadership', in G Lerner, *Black Women in White America: A Documentary History*, New York, NY: Vintage

Barr, A, 1991, *Practising community development: Experience in Strathclyde*, London: Community Development Foundation

Bassel, L, Emejulu, A, 2014, 'Solidarity under austerity: Intersectionality in France and the United Kingdom', *Politics & Gender*, 10, 1, 130–6

Beck, D, Purcell, R, 2013, *International Community Organising: Taking Power, Making Change*, Bristol: Policy Press

Belsey, C, 2002, *Post-structuralism: A very short introduction*, Oxford: Oxford University Press

Benjamin, S, Emejulu, A, 2012, 'Social justice: Learning from concepts, terminologies and theories', in R Arshad, L Pratt, T Wrigley, (eds) *Social justice re-examined*, Stoke-on-Trent: Trentham

Berndt, HE, 1977, *The new rulers of the ghetto: The community development corporation and urban poverty*, Westport: Greenwood

Berlin, I, 1958, 'Two Concepts of Liberty', in I Berlin, 1969, *Four Essays on Liberty*, Oxford: Oxford University Press

Blackman, T, 1994, *Urban policy in practice*, London: Routledge

Blagg, H, Derricourt, N, 1982, 'Why we need to reconstruct a theory of the state for community work', in G Craig, N Derricourt, M Loney, (eds), 1982, *Community work and the state: Towards a radical practice*, London: Routledge

Block, F, Cloward, RA, Ehrenreich, B, 1987, *The mean season: The attack on the welfare state*, New York, NY: Pantheon

Bookman, A, Morgen, S (eds), 1988, *Women and the politics of empowerment*, Philadelphia, PA: Temple University Press

Boyte, H, 1980, *The Backyard Revolution*, Philadelphia, PA: Temple University Press.

Boyte, H, 1985, 'The politics of community', *The Nation*, http://live.thenation.com/archive/detail/10977885

Boyte, H, Booth, H, Max, S, 1986, *Citizen action and the new American populism*, Philadelphia, PA: Temple University Press

Bradshaw, C, Soifer, S, Gutierrez, L, 1994, 'Toward a hybrid model for effective organizing in communities of color', *Journal of Community Practice*, 1, 1, 25–56

Brager, G, Specht, H, 1973, *Community Organisation*, New York, NY: Columbia University Press

Brandwein, RA, 1987, 'Women and community organization', in DS Burden, N Gottlieb (eds) *The Woman Client*, New York, NY: Tavistock

Bunyan, P, 2010, 'Broad-based organizing in the UK: Reasserting the centrality of political activity in community development', *Community Development Journal*, 45, 111–27

Burkett, I, 2001, 'Traversing the swampy terrain of postmodern communities: Towards theoretical revisionings of community development', *European Journal of Social Work*, 4, 3, 233–46

Burns, D, Hambleton, R, Hoggett, P, 1994, *The politics of decentralization: Revitalising local democracy*, Basingstoke: Macmillan

Butcher, H, Banks, S, Henderson, P, Robertson, J, 2007, *Critical Community Practice*, Bristol: Policy Press

Calouste Gulbenkian Foundation, 1968, *Community work and social change: The report of a study group on training*, London: Longmans

Calouste Gulbenkian Foundation, 1973, *Current issues in community work. A study by the Community Work Group*, London: Routledge

Carmichael, S, Hamilton, CV, 1967, *Black power*, London: Penguin

Carson, C, 1995, *In struggle: SNCC and the Black awakening of the 1960s*, Cambridge: Harvard University Press

Chambers, ET, 2003, *Roots for radicals: Organizing for power, action, and justice*, New York, NY: Continuum

Checkoway, BN, 2009, 'Community change for diverse democracy', *Community Development Journal*, 44, 1, 5–21.

Choudry, A, Shragge, E, 2011, 'Disciplining dissent: NGOs and community organizations', *Globalizations*, 8, 4, 503–17

Clinton, WJ, 2004, *My life*, New York: Knopf

Cochrane, A, 1993, *Whatever happened to local government?* Milton Keynes: Open University Press

Cockburn, C, 1977, *The local state: Management of cities and people*, London: Pluto Press

Collins, C, Lister, J, 1996, 'Hands up or heads up?' In I Cooke, M Shaw, (eds) *Radical Community Work. Perspectives from practice*, Edinburgh: Moray House

Combahee River Collective, 1977, 'Combahee River collective statement: Black feminist organizing in the seventies and eighties', in C Moraga, G Anzaldua, (eds) *This bridge called my back: Writings by radical women of color*, New York, NY: Kitchen Table

Cooke, I, 1996, 'Whatever happened to the class of '68? The changing context of radical community work practice', in I Cook, M Shaw, (eds) *Radical community work: Perspectives from practice in Scotland*, Edinburgh: Moray House

Cooke, I, Shaw, M, 1997, *Radical community work. Perspectives from practice in Scotland*, Edinburgh: Moray House

CDP (Community Development Project), 1977, *Gilding the Ghetto: The state and the poverty experiments*, London: Community Development Project Inter-project Editorial Team

CDP, 1978, *The Costs of Industrial Change*, London: Community Development Project and Inter-project Editorial Team

Craig, G, Derricourt, N, Loney, M (eds), 1982, *Community Work and the State: Towards a Radical Practice*, London: Routledge

Craig, G, Mayo, M (eds), 1995, *Community Empowerment: A Reader in Participation and Development*, London: Zed

Curno, P (ed ), 1978, *Political issues and community work*, London: Routledge

Daley, JM, Wong, P, 1994, 'Community development with emerging ethnic communities', *Journal of Community Practice*, 1, 1, 9–24

Davidson, M, Ward, K, 2013, 'Picking up the pieces: Austerity urbanism, California and fiscal crisis', *Cambridge Journal of Regions, Economy and Society*, 7, 1, 81–97

Dearlove, J, 1974, 'The control of change and the regulation of community action', in Jones, D, Mayo, M. (eds), *Community Work One*, London: Routledge

DeFilippis, J, Fisher, R, Shragge, E, 2009, 'What's left in the community?' *Community Development Journal*, 44, 1, 38–52

DeFilippis, J, Fisher, R, Shragge, E, 2010, *Contesting community: The limits and potential of local organizing*, New Brunswick, NJ: Rutgers University Press

Delgado, G, 1986, *Organizing the movement: The roots and growth of ACORN*, Philadelphia, PA: Temple University Press

Delgado, G, 1998, 'The last stop sign', *Shelterforce Online*, 101 (November/December), www.nhi.org/online/issues/102/stopsign.html

Derrida, J, 1974, *Of grammatology*, Baltimore, MD: Johns Hopkins University Press

Diamond, S, 1995, *Roads to dominion: Right-wing movements and political power in the United States*, New York, NY: Guilford

Dixon, G, Johnson, C, Leigh, S, Turnbull, N, 1982, 'Feminist perspectives and practice', in G Craig, N Derricourt, M Loney (eds) *Community work and the state: Towards a radical practice*, London: Routledge

Dominelli, L, 2006, *Women and Community Action*, Bristol: Policy Press

Dreir, P, 2005, *ACORN and progressive politics in America*, http://comm-org.wisc.edu/papers2005/dreier.htm

Dwyer, P, 2000, *Welfare rights and responsibilities: Contesting social citizenship*, Bristol: Policy Press

ELCU (East London Claimants Union), 1974, 'East London Claimants Union and the concept of self management', in D Jones, M Mayo (eds) *Community work one*, London: Routledge

Echols, A, 1989, *Daring to be bad: Radical feminism in America, 1967–1975*, Minneapolis, MN: University of Minnesota Press

Ehrenreich, B, 1987, 'The New Right attack on social welfare', in F Block, RA Cloward, B Ehrenreich (eds), *The Mean Season: The Attack on the Welfare State*, New York: Pantheon

Emejulu, A, 2010, 'The Silencing of Radical Democracy in American Community Development: The Struggle of Identities, Discourses and Practices', *Community Development Journal*, 46, 2, 229–44

Emejulu, A, 2011, 'Re-theorising feminist community development: Towards a radical democratic citizenship', *Community Development Journal*, 46, 3, 378–90

Emejulu, A, Bassel, L, 2013, *Between Scylla and Charybdis: Enterprise and Austerity as a Double Hazard for Non-Governmental Organisations in France and the UK*, Centre for Education for Racial Equality in Scotland, Briefing No. 2, www.ceres.education.ed.ac.uk/wp-content/uploads/Briefing-No.2.pdf

Etzioni, A, 1993, *The Spirit of Community: Rights, Responsibilities, and the Communitarian Agenda*, New York, NY: Crown

Evans, S, 1980, *Personal politics: The roots of women's liberation in the civil rights movement and the New Left*, New York, NY: Vintage

Fabricant, M, Burghardt, S, 1998, 'Rising from the ashes of cutback, political warfare and degraded services', *Journal of Community Practice*, 5, 4, 53–65

Faulks, K, 1998, *Citizenship in Modern Britain*, Edinburgh: Edinburgh University Press

Ferguson, RF, Dickens, WT (eds), 1999, *Urban Problems and Community Development*, Washington, DC: Brooking Institution Press

Ferree, MM, Martin, PY, eds, 1995, *Feminist organizations: Harvest of the new women's movement*, Philadelphia, PA: Temple University Press

Filkin, E, Naish, M, 1982, 'Whose side are we on? The damage done by neutrality', in Craig, G, Derricourt, N, Loney, M (eds) *Community work and the state: Towards a radical practice*, London: Routledge

Filner, M, 2001, Community development corporations: An historical overview, University of Minnesota research case study series [working paper], Center for Democracy and Citizenship, Minneapolis, MN: University of Minnesota

Fisher, R, 1994, *Let the people decide: Neighbourhood organizing in America*, Boston: Twayne

Fisher, R, Shragge, E, 2000, 'Challenging community organizing: Facing the 21st century', *Journal of Community Practice*, 8, 3, 1–19

Fleetwood, M, Lambert, J, 1982, 'Bringing socialism home: Theory and practice for a radical community action', in Craig, G, Derricourt, N, Loney, M (eds) *Community Work and the State: Towards a Radical Practice*, London: Routledge

Floyd, R, 2007, 'Book Review of Lene Hansen, 2006', *Security as practice: Discourse analysis and the Bosnian war*, London: Routledge. Review in *Journal of International Relations and Development*, 10, 2, 214–217

Foucault, M, 1980, *Power/knowledge: Selected interviews and other writings 1972–1977*, London: Harvester Wheatsheaf

Fraser, N, 1997, *Justice interruptus: Critical reflections on the 'postsocialist' condition*, London: Routledge

Fraser, N, 2003, 'Rethinking recognition: Overcoming displacement and reification in cultural politics', in Hobson, B (ed) *Recognition struggles and social movements: Contested identities, agency and power*, Cambridge: Cambridge University Press

Fraser, N, 2005, 'Reframing justice in a globalizing world', *New Left Review*, 36, 69–78.

Freire, P, 1970, *Pedagogy of the Oppressed*, London: Penguin.

From, A, 2005, William Jefferson Clinton: 'New Democrat' from Hope, www.dlc.org/ndol_ci4b58-2.html?kaid=86&subid=84&con tentid=253619

Fukuyama, F, 1990, *The end of history and the last man*, New York, NY: Avon

Gardiner, JK, 1995, (ed) *Provoking agents: Gender and agency in theory and practice*, Bloomington, IL: University of Illinois Press

Gerson, P, 1993, *Popular participation in economic theory and practice, Human Resources Development and Operations Policy Working Paper Series*, Washington, DC: World Bank

Giddens, A, 1994, *Beyond left and right: The future of radical politics*, Cambridge: Polity

Gilchrist, A, 2004, *The well-connected community: A networking approach to community development*, Bristol: Policy Press

Gilkes, C. T, 1988, 'Building in many places: Multiple commitments and ideologies in Black women's community work', in A Bookman, S Morgen, (eds) *Women and the politics of empowerment*, Philadelphia, PA: Temple University Press

Gitlin, T, 1995, *The twilight of common dreams: Why America is wracked by culture wars*, New York, NY: Holt

Gittell, RJ, Vidal, A, 1998, *Community organizing: Building social capital as a development strategy*, London: Sage.

Golding, P, 1983, 'Rethinking commonsense about social policy', in D Bull, P Wilding (eds) *Thatcherism and the poor*, London: Child Poverty Action Group

Goldwater, B, 1964, 'Acceptance speech for the Republican nomination for President', www.washingtonpost.com/wp-srv/politics/daily/may98/goldwaterspeech.htm

Gordon, L, Hunter, A, 1977, 'Sex, family and the new right: Anti-feminism as a political force', *Radical America*, 11, 6 and 1, 9–25

Gorz, A, 1980, *Farewell to the working class*, London: Pluto

Gramsci, A, 1984, *Selections from the prison notebooks*, London: Lawrence and Wishart

Greaves, B, 1976, 'Communities and power' in P Hain (ed) *Community Politics*, London: John Calder

Green, J, Hunter, A, 1974, 'Racism and busing in Boston', *Radical America*, 8, 6, 1–32

Gutierrez, LM, Lewis, EA, 1992, 'A feminist perspective on organizing with women of color' in FG Rivera, JL Erlich (eds) (1992) *Community Organizing in a Diverse Society*, Boston, MA: Allyn and Bacon

Gyford, J, 1991, *Citizens, consumers and councils: Local government and the public*, London: Palgrave

Hain, P (ed), 1976, *Community politics*, London: John Calder

Hall, S, 1988, *The hard road to renewal: Thatcherism and the crisis of the left*, London: Verso

Hall, S, Massey, D, Rustin, M, 2013, 'After neoliberalism: Analysing the present', in *After neoliberalism? The Kilburn Manifesto*, London: Lawrence and Wishart Books

Hamilton, CV, 1974, 'Black and the crisis in political participation', *The Public Interest*, 34, Winter, 188–210

Hansen, L, 2006, *Security as practice: Discourse analysis and the Bosnian War*, London: Routledge.

Harvey, D, 2007, *A brief history of neoliberalism*, Oxford: Oxford University Press

Hayden, T, 2005 [1961], *The Port Huron Statement: The visionary call of the 1960s revolution*, New York, NY: Thunder's Mouth Press

Henderson, P, Thomas, DN (eds) 1980, *Readings in community work*, London: Allen and Unwin

Henderson, P, Thomas, DN, 2002, *Skills in neighbourhood work*, London: Routledge

Henderson, P, Jones, D, Thomas DN (eds), 1980, *The boundaries of change in community work*, London: Allen and Unwin

Heritage, J, 2001, Goffman, 'Garfinkel and conversation analysis', in M Wetherell, S Taylor, S Yates (eds) *Discourse theory and practice: A reader*, London: Sage

Hill, DM, 1970, *Participating in local affairs*, London: Pelican

Hill Collins, P, 2000, *Black feminist thought: Knowledge, consciousness and the politics of empowerment*, Boston, MA: Unwin Hyman

Hobson, B (ed), 2003, *Recognition struggles and social movements: Contested identities, agency and power*, Cambridge: Cambridge University Press

Hoggett, P, Mayo, M, Miller, C, 2009, *The dilemmas of development work: Ethical challenges in regeneration*, Bristol: Policy Press

Howarth, D, 2000, *Discourse*, Buckingham: Open University Press

Hunter, A, 1981, 'In the wings: New Right organization and ideology', *Radical America*, 15(1&2)

Hyde, C, 1995, 'Feminist social movement organizations survive the New Right', in MM Ferree, PY Martin (eds) *Feminist organizations: Harvest of the new women's movement*, Philadelphia, PA: Temple University Press

Ife, J, 2013, *Community development in an uncertain world*, Cambridge: Cambridge University Press

Jacobs, S, Popple, K, (eds), 1994, *Community Work in the 1990s*, Nottingham: Spokesman

Jones, K, 2006, *The making of social policy in Britain: From the Poor Law to New Labour*, London: Continuum

Jones, D, Mayo, M, eds, 1974, *Community work one*, London: Routledge

Katz, M, 2008, *The price of citizenship: Redefining the American welfare state*, Philadelphia, PA: University of Pennsylvania Press

Kerner Commission, 1968, *Report of the National Advisory Commission on civil disorders*, Washington, DC: United States Government Printing Office

Klatch, R, 1988, 'The New Right and its women', *Society*, 25, 3, 30–38

King, ML, 1967, *Where do we go from here? Chaos or community?* New York, NY: Beacon

Kingdom, JE, 1992, *No such thing as society: Individualism and community*, Buckingham: Open University Press

Kretzmann, J, 1995, 'Building communities from the inside out, Shelterforce Online', (September/October), www.nhi.org/online/issues/83/buildcomm.html

Kretzmann, J, McKnight, J, 1993, *Building communities from the inside out: A path toward finding and mobilizing a community's assets*, Skokie: ACTA Publications

Laclau, E, Mouffe, C, 1987, 'Post-Marxism without apologies', *New Left Review*, 166, November/December

Laclau, E, Mouffe, C, 2001, *Hegemony and socialist strategy: Towards a radical democratic politics*, London: Verso

Lal, D, 1994, *Participation, markets and democracy, Human Resources Development and Operations Policy Working Paper Series*, Washington, DC: World Bank

Lambert, J, 1978, 'Political values and community work practice', in P Curno (ed) *Political issues and community work*, London: Routledge

Lawrence, E, 1977, 'The working women's charter campaign', in M Mayo (ed) *Women in the community*, London: Routledge

Ledwith, M, 2007, 'Reclaiming the radical agenda: a critical approach to community development', *Concept*, 17, 2, 8–12

Ledwith, M, 2011, *Community development: A critical approach*, Bristol: Policy Press

Ledwith, M, Springett, J, 2010, *Participatory practice: Community-based action for transformative change*, Bristol: Policy Press

Lemann, N, 1995, *The promised land: The great black migration and how it changed America*, London: Vintage

Lewis, J, 1998, *Walking with the wind: A memoir of the movement*, New York, NY: Simon Schuster

Lishman, G, 1976, 'Framework for Community Politics', in P Hain (ed) *Community Politics*, London: John Calder Publishers

Loney, M, 1983, *Community against government: The British community development project 1968–78: A study of government incompetence*, London: Heinemann

Manning, B, Ohri, A, 1982, 'Racism – the response of community work', in A Ohri, B Manning, P Curno (eds) *Community work and racism*, London: Routledge

Marris, P, Rein, M, 1972, *Dilemmas of social reform: Poverty and community action in the United States*, London: Pelican

Marx, K, Engels, F, 1985, 'The Communist Manifesto', in RC Tucker, *The Marx-Engels Reader*, New York, NY: WW Norton

Mayer, M, 2013, 'First world urban activism: Beyond austerity urbanism and creative city politics', *City*, 17, 1, 5–19

Mayo, M, (ed), 1977, *Women in the community*, London: Routledge

Mayo, M, 1997, 'Partnerships for regeneration and community development: Some opportunities, challenges and constraints', *Critical Social Policy*, 17, 1, 3–26.

Mayo, M, 2000, *Cultures, communities, identities: Cultural strategies for participation and empowerment*, Basingstoke: Palgrave

Meagher, J, Tett, L, 1996, 'Domestication or liberation? Working women and community work practice', in I Cooke, M Shaw (eds) *Radical community work: Perspectives from practice in Scotland*, Edinburgh: Moray House

McKnight, J, Kretzmann, J, 1984, 'Community organizing in the 80's: Toward a post-Alinsky agenda', *Social Policy*, 14, 1, 15–17

Miliband, R, 1973, *The state in capitalist society: The analysis of the western system of power*, London: Quartet

Miliband, R, 1994, *Socialism for a sceptical age*, London: Polity

Miller, SM, Rein, M, Levitt, P, 1995, 'Community action in the United States', in G Craig, M Mayo (eds) *Community empowerment: A reader in participation and development*, London: Zed

Miller, C, Ahmad, Y, 1997, 'Community development at the crossroads: A way forward', *Policy & Politics*, 25, 3, 269–281

Mills, CW, 1963, *The sociological imagination*, Oxford: Oxford University Press

Mondros, JB, Wilson, SM, 1994, *Organizing for Power and Empowerment*, New York, NY: Columbia University Press

Moraga, C, Anzaldua, G (eds), 1984, *This bridge called my back: Writings by radical women of color*, New York, NY: Kitchen Table

Mouffe, C, 1992, 'Feminism, citizenship and radical democratic politics', in J Butler, JW Scott (eds) *Feminists theorise the political*, New York, NY: Routledge

Mueller, C, 1993, 'Ella Baker and the origins of "Participatory Democracy"', in VL Crawford, JA Rouse, B Woods (eds) *Women in the Civil Rights Movement*, Bloomington, IN: Indiana University Press

Naples, N, 1998, *Grassroots warriors: Activist mothering, community work, and the war on poverty*, New York, NY: Routledge

National Centre for Social Research (2013) 'Public attitudes to poverty and welfare 1983-2011', www.natcen.ac.uk/media/137637/poverty-and-welfare.pdf

O'Connor, J, 1998, 'US social welfare policy: The Reagan record and legacy', *Journal of Social Policy*, 27, 1, 37–61

Ohri, A, Manning, B, Curno, P, (eds), 1982, *Community work and racism*, London: Routledge

Payne, C, 1989, 'Ella Baker and models of social change', *Signs*, 14, 4, 885–899

Payne, C, 2007, *I've got the light of freedom: The organizing tradition and the Mississippi freedom struggle*, Berkley, CA: University of California Press

Peck, J, 2012, 'Austerity urbanism: American cities under extreme economy', *City*, 16, 6, 622–55

Peirce, WR, Steinbach, CF, 1987, *Corrective capitalism: The rise of America's community development corporations*, New York, NY: Ford Foundation

Philpot, R, 1999, 'Why Bill Clinton is a hero', *The New Statesman*, www.newstatesman.com/node/135229

Pitchford, M, 2008, *Making spaces for community development*, Bristol: Policy Press

Piven, FF, Cloward, R, 1979, *Poor people's movements: Why they succeed and how they fail*, New York: Pantheon

Polletta, F, 2003, 'How participatory democracy became white: Culture and organizational choice', *Mobilizations*, 10, 2, 271–88

Polletta, F, 2004, *Freedom is an endless meeting: Democracy in American social movements*, Chicago, IL: University of Chicago Press

Popple, K, 1995, *Analysing community work: Its theory and practice*, Buckingham: Open University Press

Putnam, RD, 1995, 'Bowling alone: America's declining social capital', *Journal of Democracy*, 6, 1, 65–78

Putnam, RD, 2000, *Bowling alone. The collapse and revival of the American community*, New York: Simon and Schuster

Raab, E, 1966, 'What war and which poverty?' *The Public Interest*, 3, Spring, 45–56

Radford, J, 1978, 'Don't agonise – organise', in P Curno, (ed) *Political Issues and Community Work*, London: Routledge

Ransby, B, 2003, *Ella Baker and the black freedom movement: A radical democratic vision*, Chapel Hill, NC: University of North Carolina Press

Rawls, J, 1971, *A Theory of Justice*, Cambridge: Harvard University Press

Reagan, R, 1981, 'Inaugural Address', 21 January, www.reagan.utexas.edu/archives/speeches/1981/12081a.htm

Reed, A, 1986, 'The "Black Revolution" and the reconstitution of domination', in A Reed, (ed) *Race, politics and culture: Critical essays on the radicalism of the 1960s*, Westport: Greenwood Press

Rivera, FG, Erlich, JL (eds), 1991, *Community organizing in a diverse society*, Boston, MA: Allyn & Bacon

Robnett, B, 1997, *How long? How long? African American women in the struggle for civil rights*, Oxford: Oxford University Press

Rodwell, MK, 1998, *Social work constructivist research*, London: Routledge

Rosenthal, E, Mizrahi, T, 1994, 'Should community organizations build coalitions or build their membership?' in MJ Austin, JI Lowe (eds) *Controversial issues in communities and organizations*, Boston, MA: Allyn and Bacon

Rubin, H, 1997, 'Being a conscience and a carpenter: Interpretations of the community-based development model', *Journal of Community Practice*, 4, 1, 57–90

Rubin, H, Rubin, I, 1992, *Community organizing and development*, Boston, MA: Allyn and Bacon

Salmon, H, 1978, 'Ideology and practice', in P Curno (ed) *Political issues and community work*, London: Routledge

Seguino, S, 2010, 'The global economic crisis, its gender and ethnic implications, and policy responses', *Gender & Development*, 18, 2, 179–99

Sen, R, 2003, *Stir it up: Lessons in community organizing and advocacy*, San Francisco, CA: Jossey-Bass

Shaw, M, 2008, 'Community development and the politics of community', *Community Development Journal*, 35, 401–13

Shaw, M, Martin, I, 2000, 'Community work, citizenship and democracy: Re-making the connections', *Community Development Journal*, 43, 1, 24–36

Sim, S, 2001, *Post-Marxism: An intellectual history*, London: Routledge

Smith, J, 1978, 'Hard lines and soft options', in P Curno, (ed) *Political issues and community work*, London: Routledge

Specht, H, 1975, 'The dilemmas of community work in the United Kingdom: A comment', in P Henderson, DN Thomas, (eds) *Readings in community work*, London: Allen and Unwin

Stall, S, Stoecker, R, 1997, 'Community organizing or organizing community? Gender and the crafts of empowerment', *Gender and Society*, 12, 729–56

Stoecker, R, 1997, 'The community development corporation model of urban redevelopment: A critique and an alternative', *Journal of Urban Affairs*, 19, 1–23

Stoecker, R, 2001, 'Community development and community organizing: Apples and oranges? Chicken and egg?', in R Hayduk, B Shepard, (eds) *From ACT UP to the WTO: urban protest and community building in the era of globalization*, New York, NY: Verso

Strolovitch, DZ, 2013, 'Of mancessions and hecoveries: Race, gender, and the political construction of economic crises and recoveries', *Perspectives on Politics*, 11, 1, 167–76

SNCC (Student Non-Violent Co-ordinating Committee), 1963, 'SNCC: Structure and Leadership', www.crmvet.org/docs/sncc63-1.pdf

SNCC, 1968, *SNCC Position Paper: The Basis of Black Power*, www3.iath. virginia.edu/sixties/HTML_docs/Resources/Primary/Manifestos/SNCC_black_power.html

Susser, I, 1988, 'Working-class women, social protest, and changing ideologies', in A Bookman, S Morgen (eds) *Women and the politics of empowerment*, Philadelphia, PA: Temple University Press

Tarrow, S, 1994, *Power in movement: Collective action, Social movements and politics*, Cambridge: Cambridge University Press

Taylor, M, 1995, 'Community work and the state: The changing context of UK practice', in G Craig, M Mayo (eds) *Community empowerment: A reader in participation and development*, London: Zed

Taylor, M, Barr, A, West, A, 2000, *Signposts to community development*, London: Community Development Foundation

Taylor-Gooby, P, 2011, 'Root and Branch Restructuring to Achieve Major Cuts: The Social Policy Programme of the 2010 UK Coalition Government', *Social Policy and Administration*, 46, 1, 1–22

Theodoropoulou S, Watt A, 2011, 'Withdrawal symptoms: An assessment of the austerity packages in Europe', Working Paper 2011.02, Brussels: European Trade Union Institute

Thomas, DN, 1983, *The making of community work*, London: Allen and Unwin

Titmuss, RM, 1968, *Commitment to welfare*, London: Allen and Unwin

Tobin, G, Begley, C, 2004, 'Methodological rigour within a qualitative framework', *Journal of Advanced Nursing*, 48, 4, 388–96

Twelvetrees, A, 1982; 2001, *Community work*, London: Palgrave Macmillan

UNDP (United Nations Development Programme), 1993, *Human development report: People's participation*, http://hdr.undp.org/en/reports/global/hdr1993/

Waddington, P, 1979, 'Looking ahead – community work in the 1980s', *Community Development Journal*, 14, 3, 224–234

Waddington, P, 1994, 'The value base of community work', in S Jacobs, K Popple (eds) *Community work in the 1990s*, Nottingham: Spokesman.

West, C, Zimmerman, DH, 1987, 'Doing gender', *Gender & Society*, 1, 125–51

Weiner, T, 2012, *Enemies: A history of the FBI*, New York, NY: Random House

Wildavsky, A, 1968, 'The empty-head blues: Black rebellion and white reaction', *The Public Interest*, 11, Spring, 3–16

Wilson, E, 1977, 'Women in the community', in M Mayo, (ed) *Women in the community: community work*, 3, London: Routledge

WOC (Women Organizers Collective), 1990, *Women on the advance: Highlights of a national conference on women and organizing*, www.hunter. cuny.edu/socwork/ecco/WomenOnAdvanceDocument-.pdf

Yeates, N, Haux, T, Jawad, R, and Kilkey, M (eds), 2011, *In defence of welfare*, Social Policy Association, www.social-policy.org.uk/ downloads/idow.pdf

Young, IM, 1990, *Justice and the politics of difference*, Princeton, NJ: Princeton University Press

Young, IM, 1997, 'Difference as a resource for democratic communication', in J Bonham, W Rehg (eds) *Deliberative democracy: Essays on reason and politics*, Cambridge: MIT Press

Young, T, 1976, 'The industrial connection', in P Hain (ed) *Community Politics*, London: John Calder

Zdenek, RO, 1994, 'Toward comprehensive approaches for strengthening communities', *Shelterforce Online*, 74, www.nhi.org/ online/issues/74/zdenek.html

Zinn, H, 1964, *SNCC: The new abolitionists*, Boston, MA: Beacon Press

# Index